Whose Justice?

Whose Justice? The law and the left

Edited by Colin Fox, Gregor Gall and John Scott

scottish left
review press

Published by Scottish Left Review Press
46 High Street, Biggar, ML12 6BJ, Scotland

Scottish Left Review Press is a trading name of Left Review Scotland Ltd.,
741 Shields Road, Pollokshields, Glasgow G41 4PL

www.slrpress.org

First published 2006

Editors: Colin Fox,Gregor Gall and John Scott

Copyright held by each individual contributor 2006

British Library Cataloguing-in-Publication Data are available

ISBN 0-9550362-1- 6-

Printed and bound in Great Britain by
Digisource, Unit 12, Dunlop Square, SW Deans Industrial Estate,
Livingston EH54 8SB, Scotland, UK

Design and layout by Carla Belkevitz

Cover design by Nadia Lucchesi

Scottish Left Review Press co-editors: Robin McAlpine and Gregor Gall.

Scottish Left Review Press is the publishing arm of Scottish Left Review, the home of radical thinking in Scotland.

Previous title –
No Idea: control, liberation and the social imagination by Robin McAlpine, 2005.

Forthcoming title –
Is there a Scottish Road to Socialism? edited by Gregor Gall, 2006.

Scottish Left Review Press welcomes proposals or manuscripts for consideration as future titles. Please contact either:

Robin McAlpine (editorial@scottishleftreview.org)

or

Professor Gregor Gall (g.gall@herts.ac.uk).

Contents

About the Editors

Colin Fox is the Scottish Socialist Party List MSP for the Lothians. He holds the position of being the justice spokesperson for the SSP in the Scottish Parliament. Since 2004, he has been the national convenor of the SSP. He is an editorial board member of the Scottish Left Review and refounded both the Edinburgh People's Festival and the Edinburgh Mayday March Committee.

Dr Gregor Gall is Professor of Industrial Relations and Director of the Centre for Employment Studies at the University of Hertfordshire. He was previously Professor of Industrial Relations at the University of Stirling and is author of The Meaning of Militancy? Postal workers and industrial relations (2003, Ashgate), The Political Economy of Scotland: Red Scotland? Radical Scotland? (2005, University of Wales) and editor of Union Organising: campaigning for trade union recognition (2003, Routledge) and Union Recognition: Organising and Bargaining Outcomes (2006, Routledge). He is an editorial board member of the Scottish Left Review, writes regularly for the Scottish Left Review, the Morning Star and Scottish Socialist Voice amongst others. He lives in Edinburgh.

John Scott is a solicitor-advocate dealing exclusively in criminal cases, handling appeals as well as trials at all levels of court. He was previously chair of the Scottish Human Rights Centre (formerly, the Scottish Council for Civil Liberties) from 1997 to 2005 (when the Centre closed). He is currently chair of the Howard League for Penal Reform in Scotland, an associate member of the Scottish Consortium on Crime and Criminal Justice and a member of the Committee of the Society of Solicitor-Advocates. John is frequently called upon by the media to give comment and analysis on issues of crime and justice in Scotland.

Chapter 1

A Call to Policy, and then a Call to Implementation

Gregor Gall

Pick up any newspaper covering Scottish affairs, whether tabloid or broadsheet, on virtually any day of any week, and you can find an almost unlimited coverage of stories about crime, victims of crime and the attendant social disruption caused by crime. The same is true of BBC Scotland's *Reporting Scotland* and STV's *Scotland Today.* Even Bob Wylie's special reports tend to fall into this terrain. Of course, far less space and time is given over to serious discussion concerning the social and economic causes of crime – the social and economic dislocation that gives rise to it in the first instance – and from the basis of developing a grounded understanding, the creation of suitable and appropriate remedies. And while it is correct for progressive voices to call for full employment, better paid, decent jobs, higher unemployment benefits, better resourced community facilities, greater social protection of vulnerable social groups and the like as ways to the combat and eradicate the underlying 'crime', this still leaves a lacunae in the thinking of the left on crime and justice. This lacunae exists not just because calling for something is often an ocean apart from the achievement of it, but because even if a significant part of such a reform programme was achieved, it would be naïve to think that all the problems giving rise to, and associated with, crime would simply melt away, either immediately or in the eventual fullness of time.

The arrival of the Scottish Parliament (and justice being a firm part of its devolved business), alongside the existence of the long tradition of the independence of the Scottish legal system means that there are potential opportunities for reform and radicalism that are not present through the Westminster Parliament - potential opportunities not just to change existing law on 'crime' and 'punishment' but to re-conceive 'crime' as part of the wider issue of creating social justice, stability, cohesion and fairness. An obvious case in point concerns the regulation of employers with regard to duty of care towards their employed workers. But there are others relating to the workings of civil justice and the regulation of conduct between organisations and individuals, with the organisations being employers, public bodies, private, not-for-profit trusts and the individuals being citizens or consumers.

Seven years after the return of the Scottish Parliament, there has not been much evidence of such possibilities in Scotland being taken. Even the debate on such radical reformation, rather than action, has been difficult to create and sustain. Why is this? One major part of the answer must be, surely, the smothering of the possibilities by our own Scottish version of 'new Labour'. And knowingly or unknowingly, nothing much afresh has come from the Liberals Democrats or SNP (or, indeed, the Greens).

If neo-liberalism now characterises new Labour's economic policy then its sibling, neo-conservatism, now characterises its social policy. As the major party, it has exerted a gravitational pull on the other centre and centre-left parties (aided admirably by the Tories). But 'new Labour' has only been one, even if the major, part of the roadblock on our thinking here. Our 'fourth estate' has not provided much in the way of free thinking, the characteristic of the supposed enlightened and egalitarian Scottish mind. Occasional such articles and features in the *Sunday Herald* do not, and cannot, change this picture. Consequently, it is very difficult for public debate, assuming there are really such forums for it to effectively take place in outside those of the chattering classes, to be able to conduct an informed dialogue which then influences and determines public policy.

The left cannot evade its responsibility either for this sorry state of affairs. It has traditionally eschewed any notion that the state can play a positive role in justice. This position seems to be increasingly untenable as it is unable to attempt to provide remedies and solutions for immediate problems and challenges for those the left seeks to help, empower and liberate. Working out such remedies and solutions in the 'here and now' does not preclude the project of a more thoroughgoing social transformation – rather working out these issues may help to build the forces for a more thoroughgoing social transformation. So it is incumbent upon those who rightly decry incarceration by the state as pretty much the single solution proffered by the establishment parties to put forward their own credible and constructive alternatives because, to paraphrase Blair, the right to criticise also comes with the responsibility to suggest serious alternatives.

The Scottish Left Review Press is an ideal vehicle by which this project can take place. It is the book publishing arm of the cross-left *Scottish Left Review* bi-monthly magazine, involving people of different left persuasions, of left parties and of no parties. The *Scottish Left Review* is dedicated to creating both dialogue amongst the left in Scotland and new, critical and informed thinking of the left. It has been a home for critical and radical thinking since it started publication in late 2000 (see scottishleftreview.org).

In this particular case, the project of kick-starting some new thinking on the left about justice has been fortunate enough to call on a number of high-profile thinkers and practitioners not only to offer their views on various aspects of justice but also to set out arguments and perspectives which can begin to offer practical solutions to the issues we face as well as to challenge accepted conventions (of the left and the right) on these issues. So we have academics, who are paid to think, and practitioners who have taken the time to reflect on their professional experience.

Thus, in the order they appear, we have Jacqueline Tombs, Professor of Criminology at the University of Stirling. She also holds a number of other positions; Visiting Professor of Criminology at Glasgow Caledonian University, Adjunct Professor at the Edith Cowan University in western Australia, and Associate at the International Centre for Prison Studies at King's College, London University. She is a Committee Member of the Howard League for Penal Reform in Scotland and an Associate Member of the Scottish Consortium on Crime and Criminal Justice. Previously, she was responsible for criminological, socio-legal and social work research in the Scottish Office and and has advised a wide range of international and national policy bodies on crime and criminal justice matters. She is a member of the Editorial Board of the *British Journal of Criminology* and the Editorial Advisory Board for the *Howard Journal of Criminal Justice*. She is author of, amongst others, *Making Sense of Drugs and Crime: drugs, crime and penal policy (2002)*, *Rethinking Criminal Justice in Scotland (2000)*, and *Social Work and Criminal Justice: The Impact of Policy* (with Fiona Paterson, 1998).

Tommy Sheridan, the Scottish Socialist Party List MSP for Glasgow, has made a name for himself in starting to reformulate ideas about how the left approaches issues of crime and justice. He has taken the approach of trying to develop responses which deal with problems in a grounded, more immediate manner, and as such, he caused a stir by advocating a harder approach to knife crime in the Parliament (see report in Glasgow *Evening Times* (17 December 2004)) and by his article in the *Scottish Socialist Voice* (no. 204, 20 January 2005) as well as by defending the right of the 'NatWest Three' to a fair trial. Of related interest was a series of short contributions on community policing in the *Scottish Socialist Voice* (no. 254, 3 March 2006, available at scottishsocialistvoice.net), to which Tommy contributed.

Alastair Duff was a Solicitor Advocate at Edinburgh solicitors, McCourt, before being appointed as a Sheriff of Tayside Central and Fife at Dundee. He has served on the Criminal Law Committee of the Law Society of Scotland.

Keith Baldassara is long time resident of Pollok, Glasgow and since 2003 has been the local councillor for the area. Keith was elected as the Scottish Socialist Party candidate following the holding of the seat by Tommy Sheridan since 1992. Keith has sought to develop a constructive approach to the immediate questions facing him as a councillor in a deprived inner-city area. In this, he has sought to eschew some established left notions – not so much those which attribute to the police the role of being 'part of the problem', but rather than the police should be made accountable and responsible to the community they are supposed to serve, where this accountability and responsibility are determined by the community itself.

Clive Fairweather was formerly HM Chief Inspector of Prisons, 1994-2002, and is a frequent commentator in the media on prison issues. He was a high-profile supporter of the innovative Airborne Initiative for young offenders. Based in Carluke, Lanarkshire, this project was forced to fold after the Scottish Executive cut off its funding in 2004 after ten years of operation.

John McManus works for the Miscarriages of Justice Organisation in Scotland (mojoscotland.com), where he is the project co-ordinator. MOJO (Scotland) is a human right organisation, set up by Paddy Hill and John McManus, which is dedicated to assisting innocent people both in prison and after their release. Its main objective is to help counsel innocent people after they are released from prison and then gradually help them come to terms with the modern world. It operates an advocacy service helping innocent victims who are still inside prison claiming they are innocent. This is carried out by recommending 'good' defence lawyers, as well as forensic experts and contacts within the media to raise the profile of their cases and bring them to the public's attention.

Mike Dailly has been Principal Solicitor at Govan Law Centre, Glasgow since 1999. He was previously an Associate Solicitor at Legal Services Agency law centre for five years. He has drafted legislation at the Scottish Parliament and at Westminster, including the *Abolition of Poindings and Warrant Sales Act 2001, Breastfeeding (Scotland) Act 2005, School Meals (Scotland) Bill, Prevention of Homelessness Bill, Health Board Elections (Scotland) Bill, and the Gypsy Traveller Law Reform (Scotland) Bill.* He has written, lectured and broadcast extensively on housing and debt law and regularly comments on civil justice issues in the media. He presented the series *Buy Now, Pay Later* for BBC Radio Scotland in 2001 and undertakes a large volume of court work within the field of social welfare law in Scotland. He lectures part-time on housing law at the University of Glasgow, and provides professional legal training for the Chartered Institute of Housing and Money Advice Scotland. He is editor of *Green's Housing Law Reports* and *Butterworths Scottish Housing Law Statutes,* co-annotator of the *Housing (Scotland) Act 2001,* contributing author to *Social Work and the Law* (Open University 2003), former editor of the *SCOLAG Legal Journal,* and former convenor of the Scottish Legal Action Group. Finally, Mike is also an active campaigner for community regeneration in Glasgow Govan and Pollokshields, and is co-founder of the East Pollokshields Community Regeneration Partnership.

Ian Tasker has been the STUC's health and safety officer since 2001, following the establishment of the STUC Health and Safety Officer post after the granting of funding from Thompsons solicitors. As a result, Ian works closely with Thompsons who share same aspiration to promote prevention of workplace fatalities and accidents, and occupational ill health. Since 2001, the STUC have been involved in a number of Scottish Executive initiatives to make Scottish workplaces safer and healthier and more recently he was one of the STUC Expert Panel Members (along with Patrick McGuire from Thompsons). Ian has contributed a number of articles on the subject of corporate killing and wider health and safety issues in publications such as the *Scottish Left Review, Scottish Trades Union Review* and the *Morning Star*. He also chairs the *Morning Star* Campaign Committee in his role as a member of the STUC secretariat.

Dr Nick McKerrell has been a lecturer in law at Glasgow Caledonian University for the last decade. His PhD, awarded by Glasgow University, is in the administrative law aspects of privatisation. He has undertaken a number of funded socio-legal research projects, most recently co-authoring a report for the Law Society of Scotland and the Equal Opportunities Commission into the treatment of female solicitors by the Scottish law profession.

Finally, Richard Haley is the main spokesperson for Scotland Against Criminalising Communities (SACC sacc.org.uk). SACC is a grassroots group set up in 2003 that campaigns against Britain's anti-terrorism acts, defends civil liberties and offers solidarity to the communities most affected by the terrorism laws. SACC is affiliated to the Britain-wide Campaign Against Criminalising Communities.

Although it has been a lot of work bringing together and editing this collection - mainly because the contributors are busy individuals with many other competing and more immediate demands on their time and energy, I think the time and effort expended has been worthwhile in producing a stimulating collection of serious, grounded and thought-provoking essays. Thanks are due not only to the many contributors but also to Colin Fox whose initial idea the project was, to Dr Lani Russell of Glasgow Caledonian University for carrying out the initial ground work of contacting potential contributors, and to Lorna Bett for transcribing the interview with Alastair Duff. If at least some of the analysis and ideas contained herein percolate through to others who are in a position to act, lobby or cajole for change in our civil and criminal justice systems, then at least there is the hope of some progress being made in this area.

Chapter 2

'I'm the only one who hasn't been to jail!'

Colin Fox MSP

When the newly elected group of Scottish Socialist Party MSPs arrived at Holyrood in May 2003, we had to quickly decide on the subjects upon which each of us would represent the party. I distinctly remember Frances Curran, the then SSP Group Secretary, informing me that I had 'got justice'. 'There's a first time for everything' I thought! So off I went to the first meeting of the Parliament's Justice 2 Committee. The amiable Tory Convenor Annabel Goldie asked 'Colin, how come you are the SSP's Justice spokesperson?' I really could not tell her how we reached our decision so I quipped 'I think it's because I am the only one who hasn't been to the jail!'

In hindsight, this could be seen as a poor answer. Some in the SSP see a stint 'inside' as a test of your 'revolutionary credentials'. Since three of my comrades have spent time 'at Her Majesty's pleasure', you would have thought they would have 'got justice' - but no. In the past three years, however, I feel I have 'done time' by visiting half the jails in the country and, frankly, I would not wish a stay there on anyone.

Little did I realise back in 2003 that justice issues were to be such a major part of New Labour's legislative programme. For the first year, it seemed the Parliament discussed nothing but Anti-Social Behaviour. And for me the issue, important as it is, has been hyped by New Labour. They seem more interested in being seen to be tough on crime than supporting the necessary initiatives that all experts will tell you are the most effective ways to solving the problem before it arises.

The Anti-Social Behaviour Bill contains plenty of new powers on tagging, parenting orders, curfews, dispersal of youngsters who have committed no crime and easier access to ASBOs themselves, but no mention of the resources and interventions which have over the decades been rather more effective when dealing with persistent and harrowing disturbances in our neighbourhoods.

The point of the Bill, we were told, was to keep young people out of the criminal justice system. In that regard, as well as many others, it has failed badly. We are now jailing people because they breached the ASBO not because of the original complaint against them. Just as interesting has been the use of ASBOs themselves. Some local councils have not applied for a single one in three years, others are into the hundreds. Why the huge variation? It is because of the differing political attitudes of the individual councils, and that does not make for a good law. ASBOs, and New Labour's claims to their effectiveness, will doubtless be a key election battlefield in 2007. Prisons will not. New Labour's penal record is not one even they would try to dress up as successful.

Despite significant investment in new buildings and accommodation blocks in recent years, which I welcome, and the end of the putrid practise of 'slopping out', which is at last now in sight, our prisons remain in a shocking state. The prison estate is at bursting point as judges send more and more offenders to jail for longer terms. The overcrowding, lack of effective rehabilitation and chronic shortage of trained staff, as well as the shocking rates of re-offending, testify to a system in crisis. Scotland's jails all over are heartbreaking, soul-destroying places. And, I say that in the knowledge there are many decent people working hard within each establishment to make a real positive difference to prisoners' lives and the time they are forced to spend there.

But we should not hold out much hope for change from such an authoritarian New Labour government. No justice issue better illustrates how far to the right New Labour has travelled under Tony Blair than the privatisation of our prisons. When he was a Shadow Home Secretary Tony Blair and his colleague, John McFall MP, repeatedly attacked the Tories' privatisation programme saying that the incarceration of prisoners was the state's responsibility alone and that the idea of private companies profiting from that responsibility was outrageous. But not anymore apparently! New Labour has built twice as many private prisons as the Tories including HMP Kilmarnock and one under construction at Addiewell in West Lothian.

In her excellent book, *Just Law* - a scathing indictment of Blairism from a justice perspective- Helena Kennedy QC recounts a promise the young Tony Blair made to us all when he was Shadow Home Secretary. She relates that Blair was so cheesed off at the 'drubbings' he got from Michael Howard that he vowed Labour in government would never be outdone on the right on law and order by the Tories ever again. Now he may have lied to us about Iraq but he has been as good as his word on law and order. There is virtually no area of justice where New Labour has not stolen the Tories' clothes.

But the aim of this book is more than knocking New Labour – that alone would be too easy. The purpose is to provide a place for the self-examination *on the left* of the left's attitudes towards crime and justice. The left has a very good record on campaigning against miscarriages of justice where innocent people are sent to jail. I have played my small part these past twenty-five years in campaigning for the Birmingham Six, Guilford Four, Oliver Campbell, Winston Sillcott, Judith Ward, Joe Steele and TC Campbell, Robert Brown and many more. I work closely with John McManus and Paddy Hill at MOJO – the Miscarriages of Justice Organisation. I have been, and remain, impressed by Scotland's unique Children's Hearing system and its many dedicated lay volunteers. I cannot help but feel that New Labour would never support such a progressive approach as this were it to be proposed today. So, I hope this publication stimulates and challenges others to look at issues of crime and justice afresh and provide vibrant new solutions and campaigns to unlock some apparently intractable problems. Criminal justice issues are seldom out of the news and that will continue.

The Lockerbie case is again under examination; the Scottish Executive still faces demands for a public enquiry into the Shirley McKie case; there was the Reliance Custodial Services contract chaos; the knife crime culture persists; and the appalling conviction levels for crimes such as rape throw up sharp questions. And all this against a backdrop of falling crime figures and better recording routines. The left has much to contribute and much to address.

For my part, I feel better able to pose the questions. For example, what is the case for prison? Is prison appropriate at least for protecting society from those who do pose a real danger? Is it not also a miscarriage of justice when the guilty walk free? What is to be the modern role of the police in our communities? What are the motives driving offending behaviour; poverty, drug or alcohol addiction, violence, sexual or other power influences? Will we always have these motivations as part of the human condition? What is the correct balance between protecting our civil liberties and protecting civil society and security? I hope the book acts as a stimulus for further fresh thinking and further collaboration on the left. And I am grateful to Professor Gregor Gall and the Scottish Left Review Press for agreeing to publish it.

Chapter 3

Justice in Scotland: Retrospect and Prospect

John Scott

The work of the Scottish Human Rights Centre was diverse and often had an international dimension. Our executive committee members came from a wide range of occupations and professions. Despite that, a significant amount of our work came from issues relating to criminal justice in Scotland. Indeed, for the last eighteen years our Chair has been a criminal lawyer practising in legal aid work in either Castlemilk in Glasgow or Leith in Edinburgh. When the Centre closed on 22 December 2005, I was involved in helping to clear out our offices. On looking at our annual reports and paperwork covering the 35 years of the Centre's existence, it was slightly depressing to see how the same issues came up repeatedly without any apparent improvement in what the justice system-cum-process delivered. Prison conditions and overcrowding were discussed annually. Woefully, the answer in 2006 is that our limited imagination draws us to building new prisons.

There are numerous such examples of problems identified with our system even centuries ago but about which no radical steps have been taken to deal with them. Instead, only timid and ineffective measures have been introduced, sufficient to appeal to the lowest common denominator of tabloid headlines and an ill-informed occupant of the ballot box. Opportunities have been missed. After a spate of suicides at Cornton Vale prison, there appeared to be a public mood, reflected even in the tabloids, that something was far wrong if we sent vulnerable young women to an overcrowded warehouse far away from there families, where little could be done to deal with their problems which led them there, and nothing could be done to prevent their deaths. Politicians felt briefly emboldened to make promises about halving the number of female prisoners within a fixed period. Regrettably and predictably, the moment has now passed and the prison numbers are higher than ever.

I am never sure whether to trust those who claim to speak for large numbers of people. Studies suggest that it is not easy to fully extract a set of complex views on an area like criminal justice when the experience of different people will be so very different. Indeed, even the tabloids do their readers a disservice by suggesting always that they want vengeance rather than justice. It is, of course, easier to write a screaming headline that bays for blood rather than due process and a just outcome. Having said that, there appears to be a process of disengagement which has developed over the years. Despite more stories than ever about our courts in newspapers and TV, many people do not know what is done in the name of justice. The cases most frequently reported are those with greatest public interest and usually the high feelings, which accompany a terrible murder or rape. The daily business of the courts and the fact, for example, that more people are now sent to prison for longer is not widely known.

Many who have had some involvement in the justice system remain unhappy. Many who have been jurors or witnesses have come away feeling that they have seen justice done. But we need a system which dramatically increases the number of the latter. We need newspapers and TV to report fully, honestly and accurately on cases and issues. Where there are genuine problems, these need to be exposed but the system should not have to spend time appearing to remedy problems that do not exist.

In 1990, there was a Royal Commission in England which looked at criminal justice. It did not result in anything like a perfect system but there is much we could learn from it in Scotland. In Scotland over the past 25 years, there have been numerous pieces of criminal justice legislation resulting partly from genuine attempts at problem-solving but also knee-jerking and piece-meal consultations. Much of the time, we have been too busy changing nappies to see that the building is on fire.

Some changes in recent years have seemed to succeed. We now show greater respect to victims and try to keep them appropriately informed. Sadly, there are those who think that it is only possible to properly respect a victim by removing rights from a suspect. It is a conflation which even our Prime Minister (with a legal background) has propounded in relation to terrorism suspects.

One change in approach we have taken from England is the increased use of the civil law to create criminal offences. The main example is anti-social behaviour orders. There are many more in contemplation. Care is needed with such measures.

We need to look at the whole system and take the public with us if making changes. If people feel that justice is usually done in our courts, there will be greater confidence and perspective. We need a climate which allows genuine problems to be identified and tackled properly. Speed is important but not at the expense of doing it properly.

The Scottish Parliament has presented us with an opportunity to try to avoid another 25 years of sticking-plasters. When Westminster legislated for Scotland, there was little or no opportunity for a meaningful say in criminal justice legislation. Major changes were often tacked on to otherwise purely English Acts. Some radical reforms have been seen at Holyrood. The High Court reforms which were introduced in April 2005 have been fairly radical and appear to have had some success. Similar reforms are to be seen shortly in the summary criminal courts. We need to make sure that any changes create improvements and are constantly monitored to find if they still are producing the desired outcomes. We need to keep an eye on the bigger picture. In the past we have had the Criminal Justice Forum and the Standing Conference on Justice. Now we have the Sentencing Commission. Perhaps, we need a greater opportunity for public participation in such bodies. The Scottish Parliament has taken some steps to engage with the public in consultation and this can be looked at as a model.

We recently saw the appointment of a new senior judge for Scotland when Lord Hamilton became Lord-President. It was suggested that he might look again at the use of TV cameras in our courts. Having been sceptical for many years about this possibility, I am now less sure. Our courts should be for the people of Scotland rather than the lawyers or civil servants.

Chapter 4

Towards Decarceration: reducing the prison population

Jacqueline Tombs

In January 2006, the number of people in prison in Scotland was 6,883, a rate of 135 prisoners per 100,000 of the population. This rate of imprisonment, one of the highest in the European Union, is despite broadly similar crime and detection rates in Scotland as in comparable European countries. Moreover, Scotland's increasingly high imprisonment rate is against a backdrop of decreases in the rate of crime throughout the 1990s and its position as having about the widest array of community sentences available anywhere in the world. Indeed, despite countless policy reviews and statements accepting that prison is currently being used for far too many offenders who commit the less serious crimes, the increasing numbers of people going into prison show no sign of coming to a halt. For example, in its deliberations on the Future of the Scottish Prison Estate, the Scottish Executive (2002a) predicted a prison population of almost 8,000 within the next 10 years. A more recent publication has increased this figure, with projections now standing at 9,300 prisoners by 2015 (Scottish Prison Service 2006).

The reasons for this apparently unstoppable rise in the prison population are complex. A number of factors have played a part, including contradictions inherent in both criminal justice policies and legislation. For example, whilst policies and legislation have been put into practice over the last decade or so that imply increased use of imprisonment, at one and the same time, restorative justice practices have been promoted as have policies aimed at reducing the use of imprisonment through increased use of community-based sentences (Tombs 2005). In addition, it has become more and more apparent that policies and practices aimed at increasing the use of community-based sentences as alternatives to imprisonment have not made an impact on reducing the use of custody (Tombs 2004). Thus whilst the promotion of community-based sentences as 'alternatives' to imprisonment has been central to criminal justice policy in Scotland for some time, debate about the role and use of alternatives as a reduction strategy has intensified in recent years in light of the ever expanding prison population. For example, we have seen a number and range of policy reviews and inquiries like the Justice 1 Committee's *Inquiry into Alternatives to Custody Official Report, Volumes 1 and 2 (scottish.parliament.uk/official_report/just1-03) and re:duce, re:habilitate, re:form – a Consultation on Reducing Reoffending in Scotland* scotland.gov.uk/consultations/justice/rrrc-00.asp) which resulted in 'Supporting Safer, Stronger Communities: Scotland's Criminal Justice Plan' (Scottish Executive 2004).

For the most part, criminal justice policies that have been specifically aimed at reducing the use of custody, by increasing the availability and improving the quality and targeting of community-based court disposals (see, for example, Paterson and Tombs 1998), have been largely based on the assumption that if more and better community sentences were available, sentencers would reduce their use of custody. A recent research study of sentencers in Scotland shows, however, that this assumption is over simplistic, that the factors influencing the use of community sentences are more complex, and that offering sentencers a wider range of community sentences will not, in itself, lead to a reduction in their use of custody (Tombs 2004). Sentencers did not identify a lack of satisfactory community options as a factor tipping their decisions towards custody. Various other inter-related factors were much more influential. Some changes in patterns of offending, especially in relation to crimes of violence and drug crimes, and sentencers' perceptions that such offending behaviour had become more serious, encouraged sentencers to make greater use of custody (see Tombs 2004). Given that sentencing practice has undoubtedly become more severe over the past decade or so, reflecting (and reinforcing) a more severe legislative framework for sentencing, and a more punitive political and social climate (see, for example, Hough et al. 2003, Tombs, 2004), approaches to reducing the use of imprisonment are required other than those focused simply on making more community sentences available.

This chapter considers what some of these approaches might be. In doing so, it draws attention to strategies for reducing prison populations that have been tried successfully in other jurisdictions. It then shows how the ways in which alternatives to custody are currently conceived fuel rather than limit penal expansion before moving on to consider how alternatives to the prison might usefully be re-conceptualised. The chapter concludes by suggesting what it would mean to imagine moving towards decarceration.

Strategies for reducing prison populations

A number of jurisdictions have made the decision to reduce their prison populations and have succeeded. Finnish policy-makers, for example, decided in the late 1960s that the imprisonment rate of 160 per 100,000 could not be justified in comparison with rates in the other Scandinavian countries of 50-70 per 100,000 – and have held to the goal of reducing their own rate for over 30 years. By the mid 1990s, the Finnish rate was in the middle of the Scandinavian rates. The Germans, in the late 1960s and early 1970s, believed that prison sentences under 6 months did more harm than good and decided to reduce their use. In one year, through the use of fines and prosecutorial diversions, the number of prison sentences of less than 6 months fell from 130,000 to under 30,000 and has fluctuated around that number ever since. Even in North Carolina – a conservative state in the United States – policy-makers decided in the 1990s that, primarily for cost reasons, prison population growth had to be restrained. North Carolina's imprisonment rate was seventh among the 50 states in 1985; by 2002 it was thirty-fifth (Tonry 2003).

These are only some examples of strategies that could be pursued if a country really wishes to reduce its prison population. Tonry (2003) characterises the range of approaches that can be adopted as broadly of two kinds: front-door options, which involve sending fewer people to prison or sending them for shorter periods, and back-door ones, which involve letting prisoners out sooner. Front-door strategies range from changing sentencing laws through to changing policies for dealing with breaches in conditions of community penalties. For example, sentencing laws could be rationalised so that judges are free to use community penalties where they consider them appropriate, and guideline judgments from the Appeal Court could indicate reduced prison sentence lengths in appropriate types of cases. It would also be possible to further enhance the credibility and availability of community penalties. Existing community penalties – for example, Drug Treatment and Testing Orders, Community Service Orders – could be extended dramatically and new ones – Day Fines – could be rapidly introduced.

Day Fines have been successfully used in a number of countries, especially in Germany, Austria, and Sweden, to reduce the use of short prison sentences. Similarly, suspended sentences, used in most of continental Europe, and strongly discouraging prison sentences for 6 months or less, would also make an impact. Other front door options include intermittent confinement and diversion into drug treatment for all offenders whose drug dependence plays a significant role in their offending (Tonry 2003). Better policies for dealing with breaches of conditions of community penalties and parole could also reduce the prison population – at present, high numbers of prisoners in Scotland are admitted due to such breaches.

However, even the diversion of a substantial number of offenders from prison would not in itself halt the growth in the prison population. Front-end diversion reforms are targeted for those offenders who are already serving the shortest terms of imprisonment (usually less than a year). Recent legislation enacting more severe sentences in Scotland (see Tombs 2004) has contributed to substantially lengthening prison terms for offenders convicted of the more serious crimes and for drug offenders. Consequently, it is this segment of the prison population that is piling up in the prisons.

The problem here is that prisoners with long sentences are unlikely to be candidates for diversion from prison. For these reasons, if a country wants to reduce its prison population, it is also necessary to consider other 'back-door' methods. Back-door strategies range from amnesties to changes in release mechanisms. Indeed, as Tonry (2003) has argued, the single most direct solution that would have an immediate and dramatic impact on the size of the prison population and would not affect public safety adversely would be to shorten prison terms.

This kind of reform can be achieved swiftly and fairly through a number of existing mechanisms, such as re-establishing a broad-based parole system and generous remission programme, rapidly extending restriction of liberty orders to permit earlier release, and developing throughcare programmes for prisoners. Such back-door strategies, which can range from amnesties to changes in release mechanisms, have been successful in other jurisdictions (see Austin et al. 2003). The French, on a regular basis, decide that the prison population is too high and reduce it – often by as much as a third – through broad based amnesties and pardons. The deterrent effect of prison – to the extent that this exists – is not undermined since the timing of any amnesty is unpredictable (Tonry 2003).

More radical – both a front door strategy for admissions and a back door one for releases – is to set an absolute prison capacity limit and, once it is reached, forbid admissions except when matched by one-for-one early releases. The examples – from the Netherlands, Denmark and Norway – show that it is possible to place convicted offenders on waiting lists. Where high-risk offenders require immediate admission, lower risk offenders can be exceptionally released. Similarly, in several American states where the courts have decided that overcrowded conditions violate minimum constitutional requirements, early release mechanisms have been implemented (Tonry 2003). Indeed, the Scottish Executive, following the judgment in Napier v Scottish Ministers case of 26 April 2004 (scotcourts.gov.uk/opinions/ P739.html) introduced such strategies.

'Alternatives' and the carceral pull

As already noted, a longstanding strategy for containing the prison population has been to strengthen the range and strictness of any community orders that can be made as an alternative to custody. Nevertheless, recent research in Scotland and other jurisdictions has demonstrated that providing sentencers with a wider and more demanding range of community-based penalties will not necessarily prove to be in, and of itself, an effective way to discourage them from using custody (Hough et al. 2003, Tombs 2004). On the contrary, the experience from Scotland and elsewhere of providing community-based sentences as alternatives to prison demonstrates that rigorously enforced community orders are likely to play a part in fuelling rather than limiting prison expansion. Rigorously enforced community orders have high failure rates amongst offenders facing short prison sentences, with high rates of imprisonment following breach. Thus, significant parts of the prison populations in many jurisdictions are made up of people breached for community penalties. Recent research in England and Wales (Hough et al. 2003) and in Scotland (Tombs 2004), for example, has shown that increased enforcement of the conditions of community sentences leads to increased levels of breach, thus contributing to the growth in the prison populations. In Scotland, those imprisoned for breach of community sentences between 1993 and 2002 increased by 126 per cent (Tombs 2004). This is why the propagation of 'tougher' and more 'prison-like' alternative sentences in the community has not reduced the use of imprisonment but has instead contributed to its growth (Carlen and Tombs 2006).

Moreover, the cumulative effects of the imposition of community orders have been found to lead to 'piling up sanctions' (Blomberg 2003) as a result of breaches, and to increases in the prison population disproportionate to increases in the general population, arrests or convictions. These findings have been reported by a number of research studies conducted in various jurisdictions in the United States (see Petersilia and Turner 1990, Blomberg et al. 1993, Blomberg and Lucken 1994, Blomberg 2003). What all these studies underline is that 'intermediate punish and treat programs' have the effect of entangling offenders with multiple sanctions, often with overlapping conditions and requirements, thus resulting in 'frequent sentence violations, new jail sentences and resulting increased jail populations' (Blomberg 2003:424).

This problem is yet further compounded by the fact that a history of breaches for community penalties makes sentencers less inclined to use alternatives to custody when sentencing for 'new' offences. Sentencers generally consider they have no option but to send an offender to prison where the offender has had previous experience of community sentences and has 'failed' and where there is nothing to suggest that a community-based sentence would be any more successful the next time (Tombs 2004). Indeed, a history of breaches for community sentences has been found to be a key influencing factor in sentencers' decisions to imprison in cases that lay on the borderline between custodial and non-custodial options (see Hough et al. 2003, Tombs 2004). In short, making community sentences even 'tougher' and more 'prison-like' by imposing multiple demands and requirements will inevitably provoke more breaches, which, as long as they are backed by imprisonment, will in turn result in more incarceration, increased demands for more prison space, more prison building and so on (see Carlen and Tombs 2006).

What this means is that alternatives to the prison can only work as real alternatives if the need to back community sentences with the default sentence of imprisonment is challenged. This means that serious consideration requires to be given to the types of sanctions – other than imprisonment – that could follow breach of community penalties. There is evidence, for example, from experience with Drug Treatment and Testing Orders that the Scottish judiciary is adapting to the idea of graded responses to breaches. This kind of graded approach could be applied to breaches for all community penalties. Moreover, given the entrenched nature of the problems faced by most offenders, many will require to serve a number of different types of community sentences and other supports before offending ceases altogether. "Key amongst these other supports are employment, housing and help with addiction and other health problems (Tombs 2003). This implies the need for a more refined understanding of 'success' and 'failure' - one that recognises that reconviction or reoffending need not be the only indicators. Signs of improvement could be the key criterion of success, for example, where the pattern of offending becomes less serious, less frequent and so on. Such an approach would involve emphasising the importance of a repeated and progressive use of community disposals in order to guard against the escalator that currently takes offenders through various community sentences into prison, either for breaching the community sentence or because previous such sentences have 'failed' (Tombs 2005).

Re-conceptualising alternatives

The idea that more and/or better alternatives alone will reduce the prison population is therefore misconceived. For what, after all, is an alternative to imprisonment? How can 'alternatives to imprisonment' be conceptualised independently of the judicial view that prison – the deprivation of liberty – is the 'ultimate sentence', qualitatively different from any alternative sentence no matter how rigorous (Tombs 2004)? Legally conceived, an alternative to imprisonment is a non-custodial sentence acceptable to sentencers at times when the seriousness of the offence and/or pattern of offending would, in the absence of an alternative, have resulted in a prison or youth custody sentence.

There is, however, another way to conceive of alternatives to custody; a view that implies that we should view community-based sentences not as 'alternatives to custody', as if they were to serve the same penal aims as custody is typically taken to serve. Instead, community-based sentences could be viewed as appropriate sentences in their own right.

As I have been argued elsewhere (Tombs 2005), rather than starting with imprisonment as the default sentence and looking for 'alternatives', the starting point could be a range of community-based sentences between which the sentencer should decide upon. This means making a strong presumption against imprisonment as a common mode of punishment. Sentencing policies and practices premised on such a presumption would regard a community sentence as the standard against which any prison sentence would have to be justified as exceptional. Only if, and when, it became clear that no community-based sentence would be appropriate would the sentencer even think of imprisonment. Where legislators and sentencers face a manifest choice between imprisonment and other modes of punishment, principles of parsimony, inclusion and rehabilitation would favour a non-custodial sentence. In short, answering the question 'why imprison?' would involve showing why no lighter, less exclusionary community sanction is adequate (Tombs 2005).

The case for making such a presumption against imprisonment is strengthened by the evidence showing that many other countries, with similar social and demographic characteristics to Scotland, can maintain much lower rates of imprisonment without decreasing public safety (see McKerrell, this volume). Further support is provided by a wealth of statistical and research evidence showing that imprisonment is not any more effective than community sentences in serving most of the traditional aims of punishment. For example, in terms of rehabilitation, a large number of meta-analyses, ranging over a large number of similar empirical studies, show negative results as far as imprisonment is concerned (see, for example, Redono et al. 2002, Lipsey and Wilson 1998). Imprisonment has also been found to have little effect in terms of general prevention and collective incapacitation. Even if retribution is taken to be the aim of punishment, in the sense that it is believed that the offender should suffer a kind of burden proportionate to his or her crime, for example, to communicate censure adequately, the burden does not need to be imprisonment. A fine or community service can be retributively adequate burdens (Tombs 2005).

Nevertheless, if a retributivist perspective is taken, it is arguable that some crimes are so serious that only imprisonment can do justice to them. In the case of such serious crimes, a retributive and symbolically exclusionary sanction -prison - might be necessary to mark society's extreme disapproval. This implies that a sentence of imprisonment would only be appropriate where this aim is paramount. For example, in the case of an offender's dangerousness to others - which would require to be demonstrated through persistent serious criminal behaviour - incapacitation through imprisonment could be necessary to protect others from harm. Even in such cases, however, it has been argued that no one should be imprisoned for longer than could be justified as deserved retribution (Tombs 2005).

In making a decision about whether or not to imprison then, operating with a presumption against the use of imprisonment would mean that legislators and sentencers would be guided by whether the offence is such a serious attack on the community's values that only prison can send the right message about it and/or by whether the offender is a serious and continuing threat to the safety of others. If the answer to both those questions is 'No' then, given the evidence that prison is no more effective than many non-custodial sentences as far as crime-reduction (whether by deterrence or rehabilitative/reformative programmes) goes, why imprison?

And even where the answer is 'Yes' to either or both of these questions, incapacitation would also require to be justified in terms of deserved retribution. In cases where incapacitation could be justified the principles of parsimony, inclusion and rehabilitation would guide decisions about sentence length and about the offender's treatment in prison and on their return to the community. For example, given the evidence that sentence length is negligible in terms of its deterrent effect, long prison sentences could be reduced (Tombs 2005). In addition, in Scotland where the vast majority of prison sentences are for six months or less, there is considerable scope to reduce the serving of short periods of imprisonment. It would, however, be important here to ensure that attempts to restrict the use of short prison sentences did not have the unintended consequence of increasing sentence lengths.

Moreover, sentencers believe that the option to use short prison sentences is essential, even though they recognise that short sentences achieve little or nothing as far as individual offenders are concerned, other than for those few who might be new enough to the criminal justice system to experience a 'short, sharp, shock'. From their point of view, in such cases, a few days or weeks in prison may be sufficient. The point of a short prison sentence is symbolic; to mark society's disapproval of certain forms of offending behaviour. Some sentencers believe that this point could also be made through suspended sentences if that option were available in Scotland (Tombs 2004). Similarly, intermittent or weekend custody could serve the same purpose. The option to reduce sentence lengths whilst retaining the support of most sentencers in Scotland is, therefore, a realistic one and one that would contribute to reducing the prison population. Short sentences could either be shortened further or sentences under a certain length could be automatically suspended. The symbolic message would still be communicated if short prison sentences were automatically suspended. Sentencers also believe that further reductions in the prison population could be achieved by reducing the use of remand through 'tagging' on bail, by introducing a 'day fine' system and by use of custody plus supervision in the community (for those not presently covered) which could reduce the length of time spent in prison on medium length sentences (Tombs 2004).

All of the above suggestions would have a part to play in any serious attempt at promoting a policy of decarceration. Indeed, given that there has been no single cause of the rise in the prison population, there is unlikely to be a single effective way of reversing the rise. Nevertheless, the core of any prison reduction strategy would necessarily be concerned directly with sentencing decisions, and in particular with the decisions *whether* to imprison and for *how long*. Developing policies that make a presumption against imprisonment will need therefore to consider how best to change sentencing practices (Tombs 2005).

Towards decarceration

From the available evidence, however, the key to embedding a presumption against the use of imprisonment in penal policies and practices lies not with sentencers alone but with the quality of the public debate about crime and punishment. It is an orthodoxy amongst prison analysts, penal commentators and criminal justice practitioners, including many sentencers, that the shift in recent years towards more severe sentencing, with more active use of prison, is in large part a response to the growth of a more intolerant climate of opinion about crime and punishment (Ashworth and Hough 1996, Dunbar and Langdon 1998).

But the climate of public opinion does not exist in a vacuum. The media, leading political figures and governments, for ideological reasons or in response to perceived public opinion, can decide to attempt to create a climate in which more or fewer people are likely to be sent to prison. The entertainment industry, in developing television programmes in which crime and the prison have become popular entertainment objects, has contributed to normalising the 'prison solution' (Mathieson 2000). Governments have directly contributed to this process by legislation making more activities criminal and by specifying increased levels of imprisonment for specific criminal acts. Political leaders have contributed more indirectly by, for example, creating a climate of public debate and expectation which make it likely that judges will send more offenders to prison or will send offenders to prison for longer periods.

Moreover, much is made in the media about judges being out of touch with what the public wants and that the public hold more punitive views. Similarly, until relatively recently the body of research on public attitudes to punishment showed that the 'public thinks that judges are out of touch with it' (Ashworth 2003:299). There is, however, an increasing amount of research indicating that the public can hold punitive and rational views at the same time (Hutton 2004) and that supplying information designed to dispel misconceptions about criminal justice and sentencing has a positive effect on public views (Chapman et al. 2002). In addition, research shows that the public are more positive about non-custodial sentences when presented with arguments based on the values and principles underlying them (Stead, 2002) and when they are given information about how these values and principles, such as fairness to the victim, offender and the public, have been reflected in the court outcome (Spencer 2004a, 2004b).

Most sentencers in Scotland support measures to educate the public about all aspects of sentencing and many participate in education through, for example, talks in schools and public meetings. Most actively attempt to explain sentencing decisions in court so that they can be understood – even by those who disagree with them. They believe that more should be done to educate the public about the legal and procedural constraints within which sentencing decisions have to be made and how these decisions constrain sentencing options. In addition, sentencers express dissatisfaction at the way in which community sentences, especially community service, are often portrayed to the public by the media. They believe that there is a need to educate the public and politicians about community service, in particular, and community sentences in general (Tombs 2004). In short, the available evidence shows that the criminal justice system as a whole needs to play a part in public education in order to assist in the promotion of a more open and informed climate of opinion about crime and punishment.

The future size of the prison population is, of course, a matter of political choice. In conclusion then, moving towards decarceration means imagining a criminal justice system where imprisonment is placed at the margins rather than at the centre. Above all, what this would mean is that, instead of continuing to create more refined prison-like substitutes for the prison, a decarceration strategy would focus on trying to create a continuum of alternatives to imprisonment, ranging from reinvigorating public services, such as education, child care, mental health and medical services, through to refashioning the justice system so that it is based on 'reparation and reconciliation rather than retribution and vengeance' (Davis 2003:106). In terms of refashioning the justice system, consideration of decriminalising drug use must be high on any decarceration agenda, given the very high proportions of prisoners with drug and alcohol problems. A key issue here would be to link decriminalisation directly with the development of community-based programmes accessible to anyone who wished to overcome their drug problem. Such programmes would be required to focus not only on treatment but also on providing opportunities for supported work and training, given the demonstrably close link between treatment success, a stable job and developing crime-free lifestyles (Currie 1993). Devoting public money to work, treatment and educational programmes, instead of using it to build and maintain prisons, will have a far greater impact on reducing crime than imprisoning more of Scotland's citizens.

Note

The chapter draws heavily on the report *Reducing the prison population* which I wrote for the Scottish Consortium on Crime and Criminal Justice (Tombs 2005), and on my research report (Tombs, 2004).

Chapter 5

How Do We Tackle Knife Crime In Scotland?

Tommy Sheridan

Is it contradictory to be a socialist and still support longer prison sentences for certain convicted criminals? If so, then I am that contradiction. I remember one debate on tougher sentences and even mandatory sentences for knife use and carrying, when it was suggested that 'socialists don't support locking people up for longer.' Well, I beg to differ. From convicted rapists to child molesters, violent murderers to domestic abuse - as a socialist who passionately believes in peace and non-violent resolution of conflict, I declare here and now that I am for zero tolerance of violence. The political left has for far too long neglected the complex issues surrounding crime and criminal justice. To raise the banner of socialism as the answer to very real and concrete problems confronting communities and citizens is no longer acceptable for a movement that strives one day to secure enough support to deliver real change. We need policies for today, the here and now, as well as policies and an optimistic vision for tomorrow.

Quite rightly, the left has been to the fore in campaigning against mis-carriages of justice and expressing solidarity with those wrongly or unsafely convicted of crimes. From Paddy Hill to the Guildford Four, TC Campbell and Joe Steele to Robert Brown - even when initially unpopular, we have correctly campaigned for the release of those wrongly convicted and de-manded compensation. In the early days of the TC Campbell and Joe Steele 'Free the Glasgow Two' campaign, I was personally criticised for support-ing their cause, even from socialist quarters. Similar doubts pervaded the early days of the Birmingham Six, Guildford Four, Judith Ward and other such cases. No wonder. The heinous crimes of blowing up innocent people or causing six members of one family to die from fire injuries, including a child, motivate revulsion and understandable demands for justice. But we on the left have always tried to view crimes and convictions rationally with real justice to the forefront. Innocent people must never suffer for crimes they did not commit. Yet where are we on the left when those convicted safely of similarly heinous crimes are given woefully inadequate sentences or when those released only half way through sentences go on to commit more horrendous crimes? Unfortunately, we leave the desire for real and meaningful justice in connection with such cases to the reactionary right instead of connecting with our natural working class constituency and their sense of fairness and justice.

Four-year-old Mark Cummings was brutally abused, murdered and disposed of down a high-rise rubbish chute in the Springburn area of Glasgow in late 2004. The man who groomed him and then murdered him, Mark Leggate, was previously convicted of child abuse but served only two years of a four-year sentence. The 1,000 or so people, predominantly women, who marched on Glasgow's George Square to demand tougher sentences for convicted paedophiles and stricter monitoring of them after release, were not led by the left determined to secure change in the name of working class kids similarly abused and/or murdered. No, unfortunately these people were organised by the reactionary right wing rag, the *News of the World*. On the Thursday before that march in Glasgow, I received a call from a *News of the World* female journalist who said she was helping to organise the event and many of those involved from the area wanted me along to speak. She said, 'They think you will speak up for them.' I couldn't attend as I was marching alongside Rose Gentle to demand 'Justice for Gordon', her 19-year-old son sacrificed on the lying killing fields of Basra in Iraq. Our march through Pollok that day was sad and uplifting. Sad due to the reason and uplifting that almost 500 took part. The point is - those working class women seeking my involvement in their march for justice for Mark Cousins associated themselves with a working class socialist politician. But, we on the left are far too often absent from such events. We are against lynch-mob mentality but we must surely be right up for anti-violence campaigns and meaningful sentences against those properly convicted of violent offences.

I recently raised the idea of mandatory sentences for anyone convicted of illegally carrying a knife. I am sick to the pit of my stomach at the horrible cancer of knife carrying that leads to the scarring of faces, loss of life and ruin of families. In just a four-week period in only three of Glasgow's Accident and Emergency departments, the medical staff recorded 484 violent assaults, 51 per cent of which involved a knife. Only 53 per cent of these incidents were reported to the police. That survey in April 2004 exposes the ugly underbelly of real violence within Glasgow and the woeful inadequacy of official police reporting of assaults.

In 2004/2005, Scotland recorded the highest number of murders for a decade, when the Dunblane massacre pushed up the figure. One hundred and thirty seven people were murdered, a 25 per cent increase on the previous year and yet another indication of an unacceptable rising trend. The average number of murders in the 1970s was 86, rising to 96 in the 1980s and 110 throughout the 1990s. A knife was the murder weapon in 72 of the 137 murders last year. We have a real and growing problem which is largely ignored by the left, yet the vast majority of those killed, stabbed, maimed and left to mourn over the graves of their young sons are working class families. Violence and violent behaviour are literally killing our class and while we are ready to organise demos against the international violence in places like Afghanistan and Iraq, we are sadly unable, unwilling or unprepared to organise similar anti-violence crusades in relation to knife crime and murders in Glasgow and throughout Scotland.

I raised mandatory sentences as a possible deterrent to knife carrying in the first place. Longer sentences for those convicted of using knives against another human being are necessary, but far too late. Knowing the individual who scarred your son's face is serving four years instead of two, is precious little consolation for a young man who can hardly leave the house any longer due to the physical and mental scarring he has suffered. I don't accept the so-called knife carrying 'culture'. It is an anti-social cancer, and should be referred to as such. Of course, mandatory sentences for knife carrying or longer sentences for knife use in and of themselves will do little to tackle the cancer of violence. We need a multi-faceted approach that involves a full-frontal assault on poverty and the hopelessness and anger it spawns. Every community requires readily accessible and appropriate facilities to host constructive recreational pursuits. From sports to drama, music, arts and other demand-led clubs and societies, we have to help our young people realise their inherently rich potential, instead of seeing them dismissively as a threat and a problem to society. Investment in real training and job opportunities alongside youth facilities and youth and community workers should be prioritised. Some changes can be delivered even in our rotten profit-driven society. If such an investment strategy were married to concerted education campaigns utilising schools, colleges, the media and peer idols in the fields of music, film and sports then we could establish knife carrying as the completely unacceptable practise it is. The socialist movement has zero tolerance of racism, domestic violence and sexism. Zero tolerance of violence and the practise of knife carrying has to be added to that list.

Some argue that mandatory sentences for knife carrying, say 18 months for instance, would lead to more people being sent to jail, not a reduction in the cancerous practise. They may be right. I don't think we have a right or wrong, black or white situation here. My contention is we have to do all that is possible to completely isolate the practice of knife-carrying as an integral part of an anti-violence strategy. Alongside anti-poverty and youth service investments, we need a harsh and recognised sanction as a spur to change. If mandatory sentences for illegally carrying a knife were introduced, then only those convicted of carrying such a weapon would be imprisoned. A zero tolerance approach to knife carrying needs punishment attached to change behavioural patterns.

The use of custodial sentences within criminal justice across the board should be resisted. Community service orders, restorative justice and massive investment in drug treatment must be central to a socialist criminal justice policy. Prison should be primarily for those convicted of violence-related crimes. Those convicted of non-violent crimes should be sentenced to community service and restorative justice orders. Changed drug laws and treatment facilities would massively reduce the prison population. Far too many are there because of drug dependency and chaotic use, not because they are a threat to society. If our jails were emptied of those who pose no threat to other human beings, we could implement genuine rehabilitation programmes for violent offenders to address their unacceptable behaviour. Once mandatory sentences for knife carrying are introduced with massive pre-publicity and education programmes, those still willing to carry a knife illegally do pose a very real threat to other citizens and deserve to have their personal liberty restricted for a time. Such an approach is entirely consistent with a zero tolerance of violence position and could effect a significant and positive change in behaviour which would save more faces and bodies from being violently scarred in the future and prevent working class lives being ended prematurely.

Chapter 6

Interview with Alastair Duff

Colin Fox MSP interviewed Alastair Duff in 2004 in the Scottish Parliament. This was just before Alastair Duff was appointed as a Sheriff for Tayside Central and Fife at Dundee on 2 April 2004.

Colin Fox (CF): Looking at prisons in Scotland as they are today, what are the circumstances you've experienced where prison *is* the best option in individual cases for dealing with people?

Alastair Duff (AD): Well, reviewing the years of my experience, the vast majority of crime that's prosecuted in Scotland is prosecuted at summary level. The kind of cases that grab the headlines, people committing horrendous crimes and being sentenced to huge periods of imprisonment are a very, very small minority of cases. Ninety-four, five or six per cent of cases are prosecuted in the summary area where people don't get jail at all or if they do, get relatively short sentences ... so, in my experience of the vast bulk of my clients are of people being prosecuted at that summary level. What I've found over the years is that most of them give up committing crime and they give up not for reasons associated with the way the criminal justice system has dealt with them. Rather, they give up because of a change in their lives elsewhere, an event that takes place and, in a way I suppose you could say that they give up because they take a hold of themselves, but usually it's some other factor that tends to bring that about: they finally get a job where they didn't have a job, they meet a good woman, settle down where before they were rather chaotic and rootless, or their granny dies or some life event occurs that sort of brings them up short. I suppose you could say it's just about maturing, it's just life moving on and they grow up - they grow up and out of it. And they tend to grow up and out of it despite what the courts do to them, not because of what the courts do to them.

CF: Over all the years, do you look back on the clients you've represented – there must be hundreds and hundreds and hundreds of them – presumably they're all young men, late teens, early twenties ...

AD: Largely, they're young men in their mid- to late teens, yes, sixteen, seventeen, eighteen, up to about twenty two or twenty three. That would be the vast majority of them and as I say, most of them just grow up and out of it, and my experience of a lot of them – not all of them, and I'll come to the others later – is that I think that if the courts can deal with them in a way which avoids sending them to prison then they're far more likely to grow up and out of it more quickly because if they're imprisoned it tends to confirm some sort of criminal status for them. If as a teenager, they're beginning to get a view of themselves as a bit of a tear-away, being a bit romantic and anarchic outlaw and they rather like the look of themselves, prison will only confirm that. It endorses that status for them. You're better not to send them to prison, because a period of imprisonment is liable to blight them in terms of the event that might just grow them out of it. So I think courts should try very hard not to send people to prison, if they can. And in a way, that's the way the legislature is set up; people are only meant to be sent to prison if no other way of dealing with them is appropriate and the courts have to put in place safeguards for the accused – to avoid them being sent to prison without the court going through certain stages and investigating alternatives to custody before it happens. But nevertheless, experience has taught me - not withstanding my approach of a kind of liberal, left-wing perspective - that unfortunately there are some people who just have to be sent to prison even if it is for quite a short period. Now, I know there is a view that nobody should get sent to prison unless it's for a pretty significant length of time because there isn't a great deal that can be done with short-term prisoners in terms of rehabilitation or education or personality changing programmes.

CF: Is that because the programme takes so long or because it's six months or the process is quite cumbersome?

AD: Well, ironically, where people are only serving half the sentence, there's hardly any time for assessment of short-term prisoners to find out what their needs might be. Long-term prisoners go through a regular process of what's called a 'risk and needs assessment' that assesses the risky areas for them, whether it's drug abuse, alcohol abuse, sexual issues, social isolation, health issues, whether that be mental health, general health, psychological health, violence, anger management....

CF: All this is conducted by Scottish Prison Service (SPS)?

AD: Yes, conducted by SPS. It's quite a vigorous process and identifies the risky and needy areas and then programmes that can be offered, programmes to deal with these sorts of issues. But there's no time for short-term prisoners to assess them, let alone then provide them with the programmes they need and so a lot of people would say 'why send anybody to prison for less than a reasonably significant amount of time because nothing will get done to them?' But you've got to say then, and this is where I think socialists have to confront this and you've got to say something about it: sometimes you have to think about the wider public, the protection of the public, which I know is a kind of very bland, easy thing to say, but, you know it's maybe better to talk about giving communities respite from these sort of people –

CF: Yeah, even if it's only for three weeks?

AD: And so of course that throws up the issue of what provides the community with more significant respite or relief. Is it a quick fix for three months when the guy's locked up or is it a more focussed, lifestyle-changing program in the community which is likely to have a longer effect and therefore perhaps give the community a break from this guy forever?

CF: Those on the left would say never mind *just* dealing with their behaviour. You've identified life-changing events in that individual - it's almost like they pass this 'age', they mature, these things happen. So the question arises, 'Do we intervene? How do we get this epiphany? Do we largely succeed in intervening to get to the root of why they did it, or do we just pass it on to SPS or whoever?' You know the issue, the guy hasn't got a job, therefore, he's ….

AD: I don't get - we don't get – to deal with those issues though the criminal justice services. Those kinds of issues like employment ….

CF: So there's a multi-agency issue here with social work, health and counselling services … they don't really all intercede at the same stage ….

AD: No, they don't… but the impression I get - and again, this is anecdotal from the papers and listening to what people say – is that clearly the criminal justice system can be one part of dealing with community disorder but it's far more likely to succeed when you ally it with community-based initiatives, not sentence-based initiatives. I was delighted to hear recently about some area of Falkirk or West Lothian, I don't know where it was, where police were saying there'd been a huge reduction in the amount of youth disorder and it had been achieved, yes, by the police applying the laws available reasonably rigorously about the sale of alcohol and so on and so forth, but it also being allied with initiatives to providing young folk with alternatives to hanging out on street corners….

CF: Youth clubs?

AD: Youth clubs, sporting, get kids using football rather than other …

CF: Diversions?

AD: Yeah. So, I always felt in the past that the Labour Party, in particular … the law and order drum is an awfully easy drum to beat. I don't think any political party has ever wanted you to pretend that they're dealing with the core, underlying issues. It's actually easier - you'll get a lot more headlines by talking the problem up and claiming you've got the immediate solutions to deal with it, rather than – and I was involved with the Labour Party before – it didn't want to say that community-based initiatives would keep young folk out of jail and are actually more effective than the jail, you know, it didn't want to say that because that's too complex a message.

CF: And also politically it's too dangerous for them?

AD: Exactly. And I always thought it was very silly because it seemed to me that the kind of initiatives that actually make a difference to youth crime are the kind of initiatives that are likely, more likely to eliminate the cause of crimes …

CF: And also, you know this kind … quick fix, one-off approach doesn't work and so having failed, you have to bang that drum even louder … anti-social behaviour bill … out-of-control toddlers and stuff like that …

AD: So, in fact, the people who are causing … mayhem … the young folk who are causing problems in communities are far more likely to come from the kind of constituency of late teens, early twenties, fairly out-of-control, but they will grow up and out of it eventually.

CF: And also working class schemes and that kind of background …

AD: Yes, so they'll grow up and out of it eventually. And a lot of the stuff we do just displaces it round and about, you know, moving them on just moves them somewhere else, CCTV cameras just displaces it somewhere else, so … a lot of it doesn't solve the problems. Now, yes, over the years, I've represented a reasonable number of people but these clients have constituted a fairly small percentage of all the people who commit serious crimes. I would say that of them there's a proportion of them, who are a very, very small proportion who I would say are irredeemably 'bad'. Again, the Daily Record loves to talk about them … I've met very, very few people professionally that I would class as irredeemably 'bad'.

CF: This begs the question - you met them because …

AD: Inevitably, statistically you only have a certain proportion of the cases going and of the cases you do only a certain proportion of them are very serious and of the very serious ones you do a tiny number, probably a handful literally over the years. Four or five, are people who sick in mind that I would say 'that guy is an absolute nutcase, you know, and locking him up forever is as good as you can get'. Most of the clients I've represented ... I think of a lot of them as feckless, you know because of their circumstances, their education, their lack of opportunity, their choices are limited and they've reached a point in their life where they could go that way and be okay or they could go that way and muck up. It's not much of a choice that they make, even when it gets to quite serious crime - you know, robberies, a lot of these high-profile cases people are getting four or five years for going down to their local off-licence or their local retailer pretending they've got a gun in their pocket or going into some dark kitchen with a baseball bat...

CF: And they're all presented like they're habitual Ronnie Biggs types ...

AD: They robbed the local shop ... a lot of it's pretty pathetic. There are the really dangerous ones are ... there are some people that just have to go to jail until you can be satisfied that the risk is acceptable and is capable of being managed in the community and that's the parole board's job. But there's a group that are in the middle who commit quite serious crimes, like you deal in heroin, that's a serious crime, you cause misery to people –

CF: And the position is we can't not send you to jail.

AD: Now, all of that is true; that's it's a serious thing to do, that you're perpetuating difficulties for other people, you're feeding a crimewave and because those other people rely on it themselves to get drugs ... crime in order to get money to buy the drugs so it's a vicious circle but the truth is that a vast proportion of the people who are convicted ... are themselves addicts who just make their money where they can and this is where it comes from ... not ... debt

CF: Internationally, are there any programmes where countries step in and they say right, well, this is the six-month trivial offences category, so there's potential for discussing a non-custodial sentence ...

AD: ...may be a bit more relaxed and lenient in Holland than in Scotland ...

CF: I get the impression from an outsider's point of view that there is the glamour chain of armed robbery ... in prisons is seen as sort of, oh, that's

'Mr Big', that's the way you get the sort of criminal status …

AD: Yes, criminals do create their own moral pecking order … with big-time drug dealers next and then at the bottom you've got sex offenders, and you've got men who bash grannies and rape and so on and so on …

CF: So take us onto the characters who are seen as 'beasts' …

AD: Well, let's leave sex offenders out of it just now. As far as the kind of seriously recidivist, violent offenders are concerned I think that unfortunately people and 'society' need protection.

CF: But even where there's the use of violence, presumably there's also the one-off offender as well?

AD: Yes. The one-off 'hot blood' crime is a lot more easy to deal with because it still will involve jail but that type of prisoner is more likely to seek early release through the parole board so you can write it up as … particular circumstances … particular background, the guy's learnt his lesson, so to speak with little to worry about the likelihood of relapse. But where you've got a person who's been committing escalating crimes of violence: assaults, serious assaults, getting twelve months then two years and finally goes completely bananas and cuts somebody up in a disco or in the street or whatever then you've got to ask this person capable of being managed in the community assuming he gets appropriate support …

CF: Is that a safe assumption to make? When the parole board makes a recommendation that somebody gets released it's based on these supporting factors …

AD: Yes, well, what the parole board has to have is information about his background, conduct in prison through a social work report, and what they call a full background report which is designed to target this particular prisoner's needs, and so, if it's sex offending they'll have a sex offenders programme … if it's drugs or alcohol abuse related, then it's about family support, homeless, emergency accommodation … so you start off with the static factors and you end up with the dynamic factors … so the prisoner can argue with you, you get a sense of what he wants.

CF: What I'm conscious of is that there are 7,000 people in the prison population, with the vast majority being in for under six months and a 66 per cent re-offending rate …

AD: ... the significance of any re-offending is colossal, but the reality is that the parole board gets it right much, much more often than it gets it wrong ... well what a lot of commentators don't realise is that the vast majority of prisoners who are released on license are released on non-parole license, in other words, the sentence determines when they get out. Prisoners are eligible to be considered for early release if they're at least half-way through their sentence. The parole board does let some people out at the half-way stage but the vast majority, I would say, don't get out until the two-thirds stage when they've got to get out and the parole board's only function in relation to these people is to decide whether any additional licence conditions should be advanced but they can't stop them getting out. So if they get out and re-offend, that's got nothing to do with the decision the parole board made.

CF: Right. Ok.

AD: But, you're right, the parole board is perceived as like a liberal organisation because the public effect of its decisions is to let people out. Of course, what the public don't see is the number of times the parole board decided not to let people out. I can only say this anecdotally, but the people who make up the parole board are not bleeding hearts. Yes, they come from psychiatric backgrounds, social work backgrounds and legal backgrounds as well as lay people and they bring their own ...

CF: ... experiences to the situation. I'm anxious to ask you this question because it's the day before you become a sheriff. Why are sheriffs sending more people to prison and rejecting non-custodial disposals? What's your attitude towards non-custodial sentences? Is it a 'political' decision to send people to jail? And what about the facilities needed to institute non-custodial orders?

AD: Well, the idea that Jack McConnell passes the buck to sheriffs doesn't surprise me in the least. Of course, everybody who's in prison more or less is there as the result of a decision by a sheriff but it's not so much because the judge makes a decision they should go to prison but the system provides that as the judge, he should do that ... For example, once a person has had several chances to the pay ... I'll give you one more chance to pay the fine then that's it ... if you don't pay it ... then the sheriff is creating the structure in this particular case. So at a simplistic level, of course, it's a result of decisions made by sheriffs ... but I don't get any sense that it is driven ... by a lack of confidence in the alternatives. Sheriffs may have a lack of confidence in the accused's likelihood of responding positively to the imposition of alternatives. I don't buy this notion that some how or another sheriffs just keep banging people up and it's nothing to do with McConnell. McConnell creates the political climate in which they are there or not there.

Chapter 7

Out on the Frontline

Keith Baldassara

As a local councillor, there are many experiences to talk of relating to the fears and concerns of a community in relation to crime and all its various features. What I have found, however, is that the sharing of this experience is not always appreciated by others in the socialist movement. The issue of policing and the legal remedies under the present system are commonly decried by the socialist left. In many respects, this is justified but in other respects, there is a necessity to use the present system as it is currently constituted in the immediate absence of anything else to hand. For example, the socialist left have no qualms about police involvement in relation to racism, bigotry, violence against woman and children, domestic abuse, sexual abuse, murder, violent assault, and various other crimes, and the legal sanctions associated with subsequent convictions. Indeed, they often call for greater, more serious police action. For the overwhelming majority of the population, the only protection against crime is recourse to the police and the courts. This is something the left would do well to recognise because their call for police to act on this and that subject as outlined above falls short when it comes to more 'ordinary' crime and disorder which is no less distressing for the people concerned.

As a local councillor, I have had to deal with on a number of instances where a section of the community is justifiably afraid as a result of intimidation and incidents of violent attacks by groups of local youths or various individuals and they demand protection from this. On the other hand, I have also had to deal with an overreaction to young people hanging around street corners, involved in no other activity except having a bit of fun with each other. When this behaviour gets a bit noisy, it is portrayed as threatening behaviour - which it is not. And it is in this context that national and local politicians have jumped on the bandwagon of 'youth disorder' (often called 'ned culture') and tagged every young person with the same label that they are threat to every housing estate, community or society at large.

Without question so-called 'youth disorder' as example an anti-social behaviour is an exaggeration. Nonetheless, to suggest there are no problem areas within certain locations or communities is also a mistake and a denial that such problems do not exist. Over the last three years as the councillor for Pollok, I have to deal with incidents of harassment and intimidation by a section of youths, road racers and violent assault by neighbour on neighbour. In relation to road racers the obvious solution is to provide traffic calming measures to slow reckless drivers and Pollok has a proud tradition of doing this. Neighbour violence has had to be treated seriously and it has been essential to involve the police in order to substantiate the allegation and support the victim especially for re-housing to a place of safety. Regarding the harassment and intimidation that is ongoing, and where there is genuine fear in a specific community, then there is no other alternative but to take a joint-approach involving a number of agencies. Normally this would involve youth services, housing, myself as the councillor, the police and the representatives and members of the community.

To suggest that the police are not involved would lead to uproar and I have dealt with many meetings involving hundreds of people where this would be the case. But the key issue at this stage is the tone that is set at the meeting particularly by myself and the other agencies. My experience has shown that to hold such a meeting and just name those responsible, or who you think are responsible, is not enough but in fact is foolish and misleading. It is essential to a) address the scale of the problem – are the allegations founded or unfounded, accurate or exaggerated?, and b) identify why we need a joint-approach and what resources are needed for the area. Such an approach is commonly welcomed by those members of the community who come to the meetings as well as those from the various agencies. The meetings also allow us to reaffirm that we wish to have a community where we all can move about freely and where no level of violence or intimidation is acceptable.

When it is confirmed that the problem is serious, a community expects the police to respond. To deny this expectation-cum-request would be wrong and not only is this view held by the older sections of the community but it is now firmly a view held by many young people themselves. However, just involving the police itself is not enough. Neither is handing over the problem to the police and hoping they will act as guardians of our interests. Rather, what is vitally important is how a community influences the role the police play, what objectives the police adopt and how the police conduct its work in order to determine the outcome for themselves, the community. Therefore, what is critical is on the one hand having community control on the policing and on the other hand demanding (and gaining) resources for facilities and street activity for young people.

Did this type of approach have a success in Pollok? Overall, the answer is a qualified 'yes'. There have been no arrests or cautions (with one or two exceptions) and there has been a police presence at specific times over weekends. One nineteen year-old individual who refused to respond to the overall request of the community and recklessly slashed a sixteen year-old girl one Friday evening is currently in prison. The positive outcome here was more street work from youth services, a new multi purpose games court and a community that felt empowered to an extent. Nonetheless, a fundamental question will be asked by socialists and others on the left: 'Should the police have been involved?' The question has to be returned to, for if it is not, then which agency or persons should take responsibility for dealing with individuals with known records of violent crimes and those that have been clearly identified as being responsible for the current attacks and intimidation within a community? Overall, the outcome of this community run exercise was a community, including young people, who felt safer and more at ease. And what is striking is that young people are quite clear themselves that whilst they wish to have improved facilities to use and somewhere to go, they also want to do so in safety.

Between 2000 and 2001, Pollok witnessed one of its most violent episodes which saw the murder of four young men aged between 15 and 24. Of these, only one did not know their assailants, being brutally stabbed making his way home to a relative. The other three knew their assailants. For 18 months, people in Pollok were thrown into a spiral of violence and intimidation with scores of families fleeing due to their friendship and connection with one of those responsible for the four murders. For many young people, it became difficult to be unafraid to move around their estate freely, without the fear of violence being too far away. As a result, a project was set up after the overwhelming evidence of the detrimental effect that this cycle of violence and fear was having on young people. It was called CALM - Campaign Against Living Miserably.

The purpose of the project was to tackle the impact of the effects of violence in a community as well as the no less tangible fear of violence in the community. Since its inception, CALM has run a number of projects; Befriending, Counselling, Capacity Building sessions and courses and also an intervention strategy to tackle gang fighting within a specific location in Pollok called the Green Bridge project. An interesting feature of CALM was a peer study/survey of 12 to 21 year olds in Pollok which dealt with the issue of crime and violence and its effect on this peer group. Four hundred and fifty one young people participated in the survey – 49 per cent were female and 51 per cent male, with the majority of respondents being aged between 13 and 17 years old. The study revealed some harrowing findings. Out of the 451, only around only 40 respondents did not think that they lived in a community where there was violence. A staggering 360 respondents had either been involved in, or had witnessed, violence in their community. For the majority, the bulk of any violence was connected to gang fighting. However, 150 had witnessed bullying and a corresponding number had also witnessed violent assault with 36 witnessing murder. The overall impact of these types of incidences left more than 400 of the respondents feeling a combination of being scared, upset, stressed, physically ill, depressed, and feeling isolated and alone. A further substantial minority were left feeling angry and bitter.

What is clear is that this survey shows the difficult and vulnerable world that young people are growing up in. When asked what the most significant cause of these problems, just under 400 claimed it was 'alcohol', with a further 300 combining 'alcohol with drugs'. 'Nothing to do' and 'territorialism/ nothing to do' also ranked high amongst other key reasons. However, when the respondents were asked how these problems could be overcome, they cited: i) greater (youth) involvement in the decision-making that determines what goes on in their community, ii) facilities designed by young people, and iii) more interaction by young people with other neighbourhoods to combat territorialism. Surprisingly, they also recognised it would be safer if the police were involved in helping them break down the barriers and boundaries to tackle territorialism.

At present, Glasgow City Council youth services anti-social task force is involved in the greater Pollok area with a pilot project engaging with young people. The Pollok leisure centre is fully committed on a Friday evening to carrying out this work, providing swimming, gymnastics, induction IT facilities, web design, health workshops, dancing/aerobics and football activities. The use of the leisure centre tells us a lot about the issues involved - before young people in certain areas are prepared to access the leisure centre, which is at the heart of some of the worst territorial problems, they need to feel safe and secure in doing so. Some sections of youth in Pollok would only be prepared to access the centre if they were bussed in by the police and returned similarly. Under the new conditions in the community we have created through collective, multi-agency work, use of the leisure centre has now proved to be extremely popular. On a Friday evening in early February 2006, which I attended, 150 youths had signed onto the courses of that evening, with ages ranging from 12 to 17 years of age.

This is a positive example of starting from where we are today and then looking at how the situation contained therein can be improved on. While the example of the Pollok leisure centre is good, it does not go far enough. This type of facility should be made more available not only every night of the week but also extended to every community and housing estate. This would be enormously beneficial in engaging young people with creative activity as well as providing young people with the ability to socialise in a friendly and secure environment.

The other side of the coin to this advance is that young people are also cynical of the police. There are many examples where young people will access a park or a corner of an estate just to hang around and chat. I spoke to one group recently from Crookston. They are angry because most of them use a section of a park to avoid a neighbouring gang but they are constantly moved on by the police. Of the dozen or so that I spoke to, all of them, both male and female, had been searched at least dozen times since January by the police and they feel angry about this. They have nowhere to go and nothing to do, and this is unacceptable. It is this 'free hand' of the police to act in an unrestrained manner that socialists cannot accept. The police cannot be allowed to just arrive and stop and search young people like this when ever it suits them. It builds up resentment and mistrust and is an abuse of power. All this is very unhelpful in trying to create community cohesion. In a very honest discussion I had with these young people, none of them admitted to carrying knifes or any other offensive weapons.

The starting point in this regard is that the police must be accountable to the public and local communities at all times. This requires putting pressure on them to act in a way that the community decides is conducive to the smooth operation of their community, whether that be directly through local elected representatives (councillors, MSPs, MPs) or community councils, tenants groups or the local authority. To not at least attempt to exert some community control over the police at worst allows them to carry on unhindered in the way they traditionally operate and at best sidelines the use of a resource that can help communities.

Crime will never be far away when there is so much inequality and lack of opportunity for young people and in society at large. Socialists have a role to play in the interests of their communities in fighting for changes today as well as the further away tomorrows. We cannot deny that the overwhelming majority of people in society see the police as playing the main role in dealing with crime and disorder. It is an area that we cannot and should not detach ourselves from, but at the same time, we must be capable of intervening and taking a more constructive and progressive approach towards crime and social injustice that is more beneficial to our communities and the young people who live there. Only then we will be capable of taking people with us further along the road to eliminating the basis of that social injustice.

Chapter 8

Justice for All

John McManus

'You've got to understand this system is a multi-million pound industry and the only thing they produce is opinions. They will do everything to protect it'. This was my introduction to Scots law about four years ago. By this time, I had known Paddy Hill for about eight years with him educating me in criminal appeals at the Royal Court of Appeal in England, and I had sat through the appeals of Patrick Nichols, Mick O'Brien, Darren Hall and Ellis Sherwood (the Cardiff Three), Raphael Rowe and Michael Davis (the M25 case), John Kamara, Eddie Gilfoyle and Susan May (both still fighting for justice), Terry Pinfold, Reg Dudley and Bob Maynard, Robert Brown and Paul Blackburn to name a few.

By 2002, I was well aware of the role of the Appeal Court, and how it had little to do with justice, innocent or guilt, but everything to do with the letter of the law and those who administered it. I watched as innocent men who had served 20, 25, 27 years were looked over, almost bewildered and dumbfounded at the hypocrisy, and the lack of integrity that went along with the judgements that were given out at their appeals. The three Lords never once looked at, or addressed, the men directly when they gave their verdict. They would finish them all off by saying we find this conviction unsatisfactory; we uphold the appeal; and your conviction is quashed (see Frank Johnson, Steven Downing and Roberts Brown's judgements at www.mojoscotland.com/judgements). No mention of their innocence, never mind an apology, that this had nothing to do with them, or the murder victim, or justice, but only the law, and the letter of the law, and how they can get out of this without having to proportion too much blame on those responsible for administering justice, nearly always crown agents or experts. I also watched with disgust after winning their appeal, all Frank Johnson, Steven Downing and Roberts Brown were given was a train ticket back to their hometown and £47. This was the only help they got to prepare them back into society, and for others, it still is.

So I returned to Scotland after helping with setting up the Miscarriages of Justice Organisation in England. My introduction to Scots law was when I spoke to a lawyer representing a MOJ case in Scotland at a procedural appeal hearing, where the Crown was trying to prevent the defence from introducing their own grounds of appeal, other than those of the Scottish Criminal Case Review Case. The defence won this right to bring in the evidence that they believed would show the corruption that kept innocent men in prison. I was angry and frustrated, seeing those who uphold the law coming out with the most pathetic arguments, and angry and frustrated also for the defence trying to prevent the truth and the facts from coming out. When I pointed it out to this highly respected criminal lawyer, he turned to me as if I was a child and gave me my introduction to Scots law saying: 'You've got to understand this system is a multi-million pound industry … '. This was the start of a farce that I have witnessed over the last four years when it comes to some of the judgements at appeals which I have heard in the highest court in Scotland.

Campbell and Steele Appeal 2004

The case I refer to above is the Appeal of Thomas Campbell and Joe Steele, and the evidence the Crown was objecting to was the introduction of Thomas Love and his sister Agnes Carlton. Their evidence was eventually allowed to be put forward, but then bizarrely never heard as it was dismissed at the final Appeal hearing (by the same judges), as neither could be deemed to be a credible witness. At the trial in 1984, the main crown witness was William Love - the deal he says he struck with the police and prosecution was that he had overheard a conversation between Thomas Campbell, Joe Steele, Thomas Gray, Gary Moore and Joe Granger discussing setting fire to the Doyle family household. According to Love, in an affidavit made since, he admits: 'But it isn't true, none of it is true. There never was any conversation in any pub nor anywhere else to discuss setting fire to anything. That was all just something that was put into my head for me to go along and say that' (see McKay and Campbell 2001).

Given that we now know the charges of shooting out the windows against William Love were soon dropped (see below and McKay and Campbell 2001), it seems strange that Love is believed when rewarded with inducements, and that when he has been 'found' to be lying, not only has he nothing to gain, but has found himself hated by most of those in authority. However, the Crown's argument at the appeal was that Love was lying, which everyone but the Crown had been arguing up to, and during, the trial. Then, for no apparent reason, he came forward to change the testament he made at trial. It would seem that even after twenty years, and with all the evidence pointing towards a miscarriage of justice, the Crown was still not willing to admit that it was wrong. Even the possibility that they were wrong did not enter into the collective thoughts of the Crown; it did not even want to listen to the possibility that Love was telling the truth - just another appalling outcome. The final Appeal hearing, heard on the 14 March 2004, was to be no different. William Love's evidence was dismissed, mainly due to the fact that no one had corroborated any of his evidence. His sister could have corroborated that he carried out the crime of the shooting out the ice cream van's windows, which he walked from after all charges were dropped, after giving evidence at Campbell and Steels' trial. None of her evidence was allowed, as she was not deemed a reliable witness as she had given five statements, two before the trial stating she knew nothing about her brother's whereabouts and three since. Her last three statements were to the effect that she witnessed her brother leave her flat when the ice cream van arrived, with a shotgun, walk a couple of hundred yards up the road and shoot out the ice cream van's windows. She was deemed an unsatisfactory witness as she had kept changing her statement. However, according to Campbell and Steels' defence solicitor, who informed me during the appeal, the first two statements where unsigned precognitions, and that if Agnes Carlton had been asked about these statements, she would have denied any knowledge of them. Since Love's sister was dismissed from the Appeal, she was never allowed to repudiate these claims, nor for that matter corroborate her brothers' crime, or therefore, the possibility that Love was now telling the truth about fitting up Campbell and Steel.

The Crown's other argument concerned the pathetic questioning by the Crown Advocate Mulholland of the two linguistic experts, Professor Brian Clifford, a forensic psychologist based at the University of East London and Dr Peter French. Their study was of alleged oral statements made by Thomas Campbell in front of four policemen. Professor Clifford reiterated in his supplementary report that, in terms of the findings, it is extremely, unlikely that any one officer was able to note the comment verbatim, far less two, never mind four. He concluded: 'that the only logical deduction which can be made in these circumstances is that at some stage all four accounts must have been compared and brought into close alignment, or worse, were created together'.

But what made me even angrier was the injustice done to the memory of the five members of the Doyle family. At the Appeal, the Crown was so desperate for us to believe that it was right, and that Campbell and Steel were guilty, it did not even contemplate the possibility that it was wrong. The Crown had no experts of its own, because, it presumed, the 'facts' spoke for themselves, but Mulholland was determined to undermine the defence experts by questioning their methodological approaches and the tests they ran. He argued that neither of the two experts had looked at the memory recall of the four policeman, and whether they had written down the statement as it was said. I remember Lord Gill peering down at him and pointing out that Mr. Campbell had experience with the police. I was raging at the insensitivity of the absurd notion that all four policemen had their notebooks and pens at the ready, like a brood of secretaries, as Campbell blurted out his confession, one that he ultimately has always denied. The fact that two men had each spent over 17 years in prison, five people where dead, including a two-year old child, made no difference to the Crown - it did not seem to have any interest in justice but only in primary school pedantry. It was pathetic, and once again, the Crown was making a mockery of justice.

William Gage Trial 2004

When we first wrote to William Gage, in January 2003, we had to explain, that technically, he was not actually a miscarriage of justice, as he had not had a trial. But what we heard did not sit right, and we assured him we would monitor his progress. As in all of our cases, it is the ingredients and quality of evidence with the proof being in the pudding and the taste in the eating so to speak, or in this case, the evidence at the trial. So therefore, we had to wait until he went to court, and then we could all make our own minds up, and if Willie was telling the truth, or otherwise, it would soon come out in the wash. Well as we started to hear his story, things began to smell wrong right away, as he had been waiting over 330 days after his indictment. He had an excellent lawyer in John MacAuley, whom Paddy and myself visited to go over his case. It turned out that the delay in going to trial was due to the Crown holding up evidence, in relation to CCTV footage and witness statements. Willie's paranoia led him to change his counsel a month before Christmas 2003. The trial then began on the 28 January 2004, 690 days after his arrest, going well over the 110-day rule.

William Gage's trial was unusual for me, as I had only sat through appeals against murder before. This was to be my first murder trial, and what an education it turned out to be. Well, the trial played up to everything that is wrong with our adversarial system, and I was both angered and bemused by how the Crown got away with what I can only describe as a theatrical farce and assorted judicial ploys. Most of the Crown's evidence should never have been allowed in a court of law, as it was full of supposition and assumptions, and very little evidence, none which we could see tied Willie Gage to the locus of the crime. The only concrete evidence that the Crown put forward came from the pregnant widow of the deceased. While our hearts went out to her loss, our heads could not believe that what she said was allowed to be used as evidence in a Scottish court of law in the twenty-first century. She stated, 24 months after the brutal death of her husband, that she recalled seeing a figure run from right to left, and as the person ran under the street light, he glanced back, she saw his eyes, 'eyes of evil, she would never forget them'. When the Advocate Depute, unsurprisingly, asked if she could see these eyes in the court, she without any hesitation, picked out William Gage. And if she was in any doubt, and for good measure, Gage happened to be sitting in a glass cage with two-uniformed policeman at either side. Although never having mentioned anything about eyes, or face for that matter, in any of her first seven statements, she was now testifying in court that she recalled the gunman's eyes from twenty feet away, as he glanced back under a sodium streetlight, wearing a mask over his face, and a hood over his head.

We have to ask ourselves, 'Did the learned Advocate Depute Mackay really believe that this woman could remember 24 months later a shadowy figure who glanced back for a second, wearing a puffed jacket with a hood and scarf around his face?' As Tracey McAlroy, the distraught wife, went on to describe his clothing, curiously, she stated he was about 5'10". I say 'curiously' because virtually all the other eyewitnesses that saw the figure leaving the locus stated the same height 5' 10"ish. But William Gage is 6'2"! Another three witnesses also went on to describe a puffed jacket fleeing the locus. I noted the shape of jacket, as the jacket the Crown produced of that worn by the killer was a thin black cagoule.

William Gage's trial shocked me to the core: I witnessed a man being sent down for twenty years on virtually no evidence, by a jury who took less than two hours to decide his fate, and the only evidence was the widow recalling someone's eyes two years later. It was complete nonsense. Even his own defence argued with me that the eye identification was valid evidence in a Scots court. It would have been laughable, if it where not so serious.

Then there was Gage's alibi witness, Anne Ross, who was discredited during the trial by the Crown on arguments that were unfounded in facts and were detrimental, and seriously prejudicial to William Gage's defence. At the trial, it was eluded that Ms. Ross was a discreditable witness, due to confusion over times and dates of entry in her diary, particularly in relation to the times of an entry on the 15 February 2002 in which she we went to see the film, *Oceans Eleven*, at the Quay leisure complex. Whilst under cross examination from the Crown, and having been informed about the time of a phone call at 20.53pm, she was asked how could she be at the cinema with Mr. Gage and receive a call from him at the 20.53pm. She stated she must have been mistaken about the starting time of the film, and that it was later than the 8.00pm/8.15pm timeframe she recalled from two years earlier. Anne Ross did not have to put her private and personal life out into the public domain to prove what she was saying was the truth, and then to be berated and called a liar, at a murder trial and in a court of law. We kept asking ourselves 'If she's telling the truth, then what time did *Oceans Eleven* start at the Quay on the 15 February?' Did anyone check? I visited the Mitchell Library the following night after the trial ended, pulled out the Evening Times and tracked down the cinema listings. The times for *Oceans Eleven* that night went as follows: the first evening showing was at 6.45pm, was too early, with the two later showings were 9.00pm and 9.30pm. She could have made it easily to both of them. The problem with the call at 20.53pm and the 'How could you take a call if you were at the pictures?' as the Advocate Depute accused her of, was what she had stated in court 'that she must have been mistaken about the time' and that it was Gage down stairs to pick her up to take her to the pictures. As she said, she did not want Willie to meet her kids because 'it was a fun relationship'. At the trial, Ms. Ross was accused of lying, where in fact she was simply mistaken about times of a movie from two years previous. Surely, if the jury had known this, they might have come back with a quite different verdict.

After two weeks and all the evidence heard, flimsy and circumstantial as it was, we were left with the judge's summation. In his summation, Lord Emslie kept referring to the high standard of proof, and of it having to show beyond reasonable doubt, as well as the burden of proof being on the Crown, and of the high standards required by the Crown. He spoke of corroboration coming from more than one source and went on to mention twice more about the evidence being beyond reasonable doubt. He could not have been clearer in his directions. He all but told them to perform on the strength of evidence, either guilty or not proven. This issue is not just about the conviction of William Gage, but about the Scottish judicial system as a whole. The last time we had witnessed such a farce was the conviction of Barry George in England, a man of limited intelligence, who was convicted on purely circumstantial evidence, for the assassination of Jill Dando. At the time, Paddy Hill could see what was coming: he told everyone that there had been a fundamental shift in English law that went right back to the Magna Carta. That the onus on being innocent until proven guilty, with evidence that shows beyond reasonable doubt, now no longer existed, and that the real onus is now on the innocent to prove their innocence. On the 14th March 2006 at a procedural appeal hearing, the appeal judges refused to allow new evidence to be put forward and have dismissed his appeal out of hand. Willie Gage will now have to apply to the Scottish Criminal Case Review Commission, and is looking at least another 4 years in prison. I have no doubt that William Gage will eventually win his appeal, and the question then will not be about his innocence, but why this case was ever brought to court on these charges with the lack of evidence in the first place.

Stuart Gair's Appeal

Stuart Gair's appeal was one of the strangest appeal hearings (and which is still ongoing) that both Paddy Hill and myself had ever witnessed. It was divided into two halves, with a judgement meted out on part of the defence argument on 7 June 2005. It could be argued that the evidence that failed was the strongest submission of his grounds for his appeal. This ruling of Stuart Gair's appeal against murder at the High Court of Judiciary in Edinburgh was presided over by the then Lord Justice General, Lord Cullen, and once again it was as perverse as it was insulting to one's intelligence. The rejected part of the argument for Gair's grounds of appeal, with which this opinion was concerned, related to the five witnesses that had come forward, and of which four gave evidence at the original trial. The four witnesses where now claiming that the evidence they gave at trial was false, and was said to be so as a result of the duress, threats and intimidation they were put under by the police. However, according to three Law Lords, 'each of the witnesses have been subject to pressure to exonerate the appellant' - that is to say, and this was how it was read by the journalists involved, that journalists and a campaigner had pressurised witnesses to come forward to the Appeal Court and make false allegations against senior policemen. The only article written about this opinion was by the investigative journalist, Eamonn O'Neill, on June 17 2005 in the *Herald*.

This case goes back to August 1989 when Stuart Gair was convicted for the murder of Peter Smith. Most of the witnesses were young working class males who said they saw Gair in the vicinity at the time of Smith's murder. There had been a number of vicious assaults on homosexuals in Glasgow around this time, and this seemed to be the homophobic fatality waiting to happen. Gair was arrested days later following the discovery on April 11 of a bleeding Mr Smith slumped at the bottom of the steps of the St. Vincent Street's gents' lavatories. A police investigation followed and a trial took place, which resulted in Stuart Gair's conviction for the murder. This was a homophobic murder, but witnesses have since come forward to allege that homophobia was then used to set up an innocent man. The decision by three Appeal Court judges not only took the place of a decision of a jury, which according to the House of Lords in the Pendelton case in 2001, was not in their jurisdiction. But, it also contained the subtle hinting of criminal conspiracy by journalists and campaigners to pervert the course of justice in pressurising Crown witnesses to make 'false' accusations against the police. What is also worrying is whether this has set a precedent in relation to getting other cases of convicted people claiming their innocence referred back to the Appeal Court. Does this mean that no matter how many witnesses come forward to say they were pressurised into making false statements, will the Scottish Criminal Cases Review Commission (SCCRC) now refuse to send their cases back to the Appeal Court because of this judgement? Another very worrying precedent set.

As we wait to hear their final judgement, my heart goes out to Stuart Gair whose life has spiralled from one catastrophe to the next. Waiting six years on interim liberation, he has found himself back in prison twice for drug offences, and then released back into society with no support for the many problems he has developed over these harrowing years as he tries to clear his name and end his nightmare.

Steven Johnston and Billy Allison's Appeal

In this appeal, the Crown's case rested on the belief that Steven Johnston and Billy Allison killed Andrew Forsyth in a frenzied attack on 3 November 1995, six days before the body was discovered on Thursday 9th November. During the trial, the jury was told that 'to bring home a conviction against Johnston and Allison, the deceased would require to have died on Friday, November 3rd'. But in its statement of reason in 2001, the SCCRC – which looks into alleged miscarriages of justice – revealed that it traced up to nine witnesses who claimed to have seen the deceased after the date the police claimed that Johnston and Allison had killed him. Three of these witnessed actually spoke to Forsyth. Each of them told the police during the murder investigation that they had seen Forsyth alive after November 3. Despite this, most of their statements were never passed on by police to the Procurators Fiscal Office, and, therefore, their evidence was never heard at trial. Michael Healy, a shopkeeper tracked down by the SCCRC, claimed that Forsyth, whom he knew, came into his shop on Saturday November 4, bought a newspaper and asked about bus times. Mhairi Cormack, a housing officer, said that she went to the dead man's house on Tuesday November 7, and looked through the front window – directly at the spot where his body was found – but could not see anything suspicious. Michael Franklin, said he had a drink with Forsyth at Jinty's bar on Wednesday, November 8 – the day before his body was discovered. Karen Wheelright also told police at the time that she had seen Forsyth in the street after the 3 November.

The report by the SCCRC states: 'The commission has found it difficult to conclude other than the police took it upon themselves to filter out the existence of witnesses whose evidence might point to the deceased having been alive after November 3. ... The commission also believes that the defence put forward, on behalf of Mr. Johnston, would have been presented in different terms had counsel been aware of the full extent of the sightings of the deceased after November 3. These actions by the police resulted in the jury not being made aware of the full timescale and range of movements of the deceased in the days immediately following the supposed date of his death' (from SCCRC Steven Johnson Statement of Reason for his appeal).

Johnston and Allison's appeal, which started on the 4 November 2005, was the most remarkable and transparent appeal I have had the pleasure to witness. Witness after witness, stood in the court, even after ten years, were still positive that Drew Forsyth was still alive after the 3 November - not only were there sightings, but three of the witnesses had actually spoken to Mr.

Forsyth after the date of death, according to the police. But the real revelation was the testament of the Senor Investigating Officer (SIO) DCI Richard Munro - he was in the dock for three days. It was not only Bert Kerrigan QC, for Johnston, who was giving him a grilling, but also the three Law Lords. At one point, early into Munro's cross examination, Lord Gill had to stop the proceedings and pointed out to Munro that 'to every question you've been asked so far, you've either replied it 'wasn't me or it was somebody else'. You were the SIO, ultimately the buck stops with you'. Ex-DCI Munro was such a reluctant witness. When Munro was asked about a letter that Johnson's defence had received in April 1996, from the then deputy Chief Constable, Graham Bennett, of the Fife Constabulary, about an internal inquiry, he denied any knowledge of statements not being handed over to the Procurator Fiscal. When Munro was asked at the appeal if he took part in this internal inquiry, he stated he could not remember, or he was not sure. Even the Lords where exasperated by this reply.

Once again it was pointed out to him that since he was leading the investigation, surely, if there had been an inquiry about the investigation that he was the head of, it stood to reason that he would have taken part in any internal investigations. To this, he shrugged his shoulders and just agreed. On the last day of his evidence, again ex-DCI Munro had to be warned about his prevaricating attitude when Lord Gill, Scotland's second most senior judge, told him, 'Let's have some straight answers to some straight questions'. One of the investigating officers, DI Chatham, admitted at the appeal in court that the senior officer who was heading the case, DCI Richard Munro, was the 'prime suspect' for changing the statement which he, DI Chatham, had taking from the publican, John Thow. Lord Gill told him, 'Inspector, you are the person in whose handwriting the statement is made and you now have in front of you a version of that statement which is plainly doctored'. In response, DI Chatham said 'I can only assume it was Mr. Munro or the office manager who was responsible.' He also told the Appeal Court that a statement he took from Michael Franklin, who reported seeing the victim alive after the date he was supposedly murdered, must have been altered as it went through police computer systems.

Appeal Court judges heard from a string of senior officers within Fife CID who admitted glaring malpractice during enquires into the death of Drew Forsyth. Sergeant Lyndsay Black told the Appeal Court that he did not know why a statement he took from a witness who claimed to have seen Forsyth on the week he supposedly died was marked 'not relevant'. Sergeant Black said, 'It seems relevant to me. It wasn't me who marked that 'not relevant''. Mr. Kerrigan QC said another statement taken by Detective Constable Amanda Given had not been passed on to the Procurator Fiscal and appeared to have 'disappeared into the ether'. She said 'If this statement never made it to the Procurator Fiscal, I can't explain that'.

When asked by Lord Johnson, 'why in heaven's didn't he pass it on to the PF?', ex-DCI Munro told the Appeal Court that, although the statements concerning sightings after 3 November 1995 were not passed over to the prosecutors, he does recall a conversation where he mentioned them to the Procurator Fiscal. However, the last day of the appeal was to see the former Dunfermline Procurator Fiscal, Robert Hamilton, called to give evidence. He told the court he could not recall being told of these statements, and it was ten years later. Bert Kerrigan cleverly asked him, if a conversation about post-death sightings had occurred, what action would he have then taken. Mr. Hamilton replied that he would have taken actions to have the statements sent over immediately. When asked 'and did you ever take these actions?', it became obvious by Mr. Hamilton's embarrassment that Munro had lied to the Appeal Court. We ran out of time for the summations, and Johnston and Allison had to go back to prison for another two months until the court could find a suitable time to resume the proceedings. On the 14 December 2005, Billy Allison and Steven Johnston were released after ten torturous years fighting to prove their innocence. If the summations are anything to go by and what was expressed in the court, it is not a case of whether Steven and Billy are innocent, but more who is responsible for this criminal conspiracy. As Lord Gill asked Mr. Kerrigan, on the last day of their appeal, 'how high a rank does he think this cover up goes?'

Billy Allison and Steven Johnston had their convictions quashed and were proclaimed a miscarriage of justice on the 17 March 2006. In their judgement, the presiding judge Lord Gill remarked of the seven officers who gave evidence at the appeal, 'With the exception of WPC Givan, the other officers from the enquiry team who gave evidence did not impress us. There is no evidence directly implicating any of them individually in the suppression or alteration of statements; but, despite the senior ranks that some of them now hold, we were not satisfied that they told us the whole truth.' At the end of the trial, the Crown office has opened up an investigation to be carried out by the Lothian and Borders Police into the handling of this case by Munro and officers of the Fife Constabulary. Hopefully, we will see justice, and convictions will be brought against these corrupt police officers. We shall soon find out, but I won't hold my breath for an honest and positive outcome. From our collective experiences in the past, it would seem that when it comes to the judging of those in positions of authority, they will never allow their own to be judged by the same rule of law that governs us, the public, no matter how corrupt they have been in perverting the course of justice.

Conclusion

The cases I have dealt with in this chapter show that no longer can Scottish justice and the legal system in Scotland be assumed to be untainted by the same type of stains that have tarnished and undermined justice and the legal system in England and Wales, through the cases of the Birmingham Six, the Guildford Four and the Cardiff Three to mention but a few. Clearly, we are not all 'Jock Tamson's bairn's' under the law. Our First Minister has stated in the Shirley McKie case that it was an 'honest mistake' – well, there was no 'honest' mistake in the fitting up of the cases discussed above. In the name of justice, and for our human rights, we now need an open and public inquiry into the operation and principles of the Scottish judicial system. We need to set up an independent body to regulate and monitor all our judicial, legal and police bodies, in order to ensure these malpractices of malfeasance, expediency or tunnel vision no longer continue. We need such an inquiry to create the opportunity to help build a real, modern democratic police and judicial system in Scotland for, as Martin Luther King commented, 'An injustice anywhere is a threat to justice everywhere'.

Note

The background and further details on the cases discussed in this chapter can be found on the MOJO (Scotland) website (www.mojoscotland.com) and the book by journalist Ron McKay with Thomas, *Indictment: Trial by Fire*, is essential reading to understand the full background and content of that particular case.

Chapter 9

The Need for Reform in Scottish Prisons

Clive Fairweather

The term 'penal reform' has echoes which stretch back over the centuries to when a number of notable reformers like John Howard and Elizabeth Frye campaigned against the poor and even barbaric conditions which existed in a number of prisons across Britain. Yet, if any of these worthy folk were able, today, to step inside somewhere like Ross Hall at HM Prison and Youth Offender's Institution Cornton Vale and view the conditions that now persist, they would shake their head in utter disbelief for so great have been the advances in penal conditions in recent years. Indeed, they might question why anyone (such as this writer) would still be pressing for reform when such an excellent model existed. After all, this brand spanking new multi-million hall was designed specifically with female remand prisoners in mind, and at various points in the day its (mainly) young women prisoners can be seen in track suits and trainers, in open association, chatting to each other, whilst staff look on from a central vestibule, flanked by spacious glass windows. Close by a state of the art medical centre has also been established. Everything appears to be being done to meet the needs of society and its prisoners, so maybe penal reformers would do better to be chasing their state pension rather than railing against the conditions which clearly have benefited from the many bitter lessons of the recent and distant past?

Looking Beyond, and Beneath, the Superficial

Yet, if the same caring individuals were to spend just a little longer actually talking to and, more importantly, listening to these women, and perhaps looking into some of the other blocks at this campus-like institution, they would surely come to this gut wrenching conclusion. And this is that far from there having been a heartening revolution in prison conditions since Victorian times, something has, instead, gone horribly wrong. They might start with the mind numbing number of women in jail for a start. Whereas in their 'unenlightened' day, and even as late as the 1960s, there would have been only a handful of unfortunate women being incarcerated, today Cornton Vale, despite its airy new Remand Hall, is bulging at the seams.

There are now over 300 women in this Stirlingshire institution - double the number since I was first appointed as HMP Chief Inspector, and most having been imprisoned for relatively petty crimes. Moreover, most, if not all, of these women have major addiction problems and backgrounds of physical and mental abuse.

Elsewhere, a new wing has had to be established at Greenock prison to cater for the sheer number of women flooding out of the courts from all over Scotland, in addition to those established at three other Scottish prisons. Far from these often bedraggled women presenting a danger to society, the majority pose a far greater danger to themselves, with many of them attempting, and sometimes succeeding, in hanging themselves. Small wonder that one of my earlier reports on Cornton Vale described it as a mixture 'of psychiatric ward, drug clinic and casualty clearing station' which would still fit the reality of all the new bricks and mortar which have gone into the erection of brand spanking new Ross Hall.

Here, at the Women's Prison in Scotland, and there are similar echoes at many other jails, it is painfully apparent to even the most casual of observers, that the need for penal reform is quite overwhelming and quite frankly, much greater than in Howard's and Frye's day. The number of damaged women being imprisoned for petty crime is a national disgrace, and as a society, after all these years of so-called 'debate', we still do not appear to have any real consensus that incarceration should be reserved for only the most dangerous and serious of male or female offenders. Not that the Scottish Executive has not come to much the same conclusions, and notwithstanding the various efforts by the newly founded Scottish Parliament to try and reverse this hugely wasteful and costly situation. Instead, despite much earnest hand wringing, and talk of 'meaningful' alternatives to custody, sentences are getting longer and in addition the prison population across Scotland is set to continue increasing, year on year - 5,000 in 1994, 7,000 in 2003/4 and forecast as 8,000 plus in less than six years time. This harrowing trend is occurring against the backdrop of a steadily declining birthrate, and it is said, a general drop in recorded serious crime. Thus, despite an expensive prison refurbishment and building programme, set against staff reductions and cost cutting, there is every danger that these institutions - and of course our society, will silt up, as once more they become virtual human cages.

Politicians and Prisons

The universal truth, repeated to me so many times by sighing politicians is that 'there are precious few votes in prisons'. Thus, until (if ever) the public put the appropriate pressure on them, the upwards trend in creating human zoos looks set to continue. The root of this very unhappy situation is almost certainly a causal link between the comparative 'health' and wealth of Scottish society, more especially in the Central Belt. As the gap between the 'haves' and the 'have nots' increases, so there seems to be a higher imprisonment rate, a fact that has been observed elsewhere in the world (and we need look no further than the USA for confirmation of this). Somewhere, in between the public and the politicians, the fiercely independent judiciary here in Scotland has detected the punitive mood and the results are very soon clogging up the (now privatized) prison vans. These 'results' may wear tracksuits and trainers (like the female remands at Cornton Vale) and they may come from homes which have satellite TV. Yet, the common denominator seems to be boredom amongst youths on housing estates, alcohol-fuelled violence, theft, prostitution etc to feed a burgeoning drug habit and other forms of mainly street crime. Equally depressing, almost half (more, the younger they are) will be unable to overcome the many obstacles and stigma which society places in their way after even a short prison sentence, and will go on to commit further crimes in order to feed their various habits. This is the so-called 'revolving door'. The public often complain that 'prison is far too soft nowadays' and who knows if they are right, but the effects of having been imprisoned in a society which needs an ever dwindling work force is much tougher than in Victorian times. For many, prison is for life or certainly the productive part of it.

Progress and Remedy

In other areas, however, the outlook is not quite so depressing. For example, over the last 15 years, there has been a gradual, and more recently escalating effort, to improve the building fabric of Scottish prisons. Several old or unsuitable institutions were even closed at the turn of the millennium (Longriggend, Dungavel, Penninghame etc) whilst in cell lavatories have been installed at Barlinnie, Edinburgh, Perth and Polmont, to name but a few. One completely new prison has been built at Kilmarnock, since 1999, and is now privately run. Two more are likely to be built within the next two years, although at the time of writing, it is not yet known whether they will be privately- or publicly-managed. Once modernisation is complete at Perth, Peterhead and possibly Aberdeen, within the next few years, the Scottish Prison Service (SPS) will be able to boast, rightly, that all its prison buildings will be fit for purpose, as is so eminently the case described already at Ross Hall in Cornton Vale.

This purpose must surely be the secure custody of serious criminals. In this respect, writing in my final *Annual Report*, I commented that so far as long-term offenders were concerned, 'the SPS appeared to tackle, in a rationale way, some of the factors that can lead to criminal behaviour'. Similarly, there has not been a successful escape by a serious offender from within any of the SPS's closed establishments since 1998, such that I could conclude, that whilst more could always be done for this difficult group, by and large the SPS had this type of prisoner 'sorted.' The creation of a National Induction Centre at HMP Shotts in the mid 1990s, which prepared long-termers for their sentence had also been an inspired experiment, and which has greatly reduced the temperature in long-term jails across Scotland.

At the other end of the scale to these 600-800 individuals, and in the same report, I was able to observe that at long last, those being held on remand (i.e., either not convicted or sentenced) and who account for about 14 per cent of the overall daily penal population, were being housed in uniformly decent conditions (probably for the first time in two centuries). This, therefore, leaves 4,000 plus prisoners as the future target for penal reform, ranging from about 1,500 short-termers (serving sentences of less than one year) to a similar number serving four to less than ten years. As the SPS is unable to deal with the short-termers' offending behaviour 'in any coherent way', either due to shortages of staff or just the basic lack of time, my conclusion was that jailing this group was largely a waste of everyone's time. 'Reform' should really be focussing, therefore, on the 2,000-odd prisoners serving sentences of one year upwards. Other areas are more encouraging, as follows;

Safety

It would appear that after a very worrying period in the 1990s, Scottish prisons are becoming safer. For example, the suicide rate has been, and not before time, dropping - down to 11 in 2000-2001, and again the following year, from an annual toll as high as 17. During my eight years as HM Chief Inspector, some 137 unfortunate individuals hanged themselves, whereas in the 63 years before judicial hanging was finally ended in Scotland, there had been 35 executions. This number of eleven is still far too many, but SPS staff deserve congratulations on achieving such a dramatic reduction in the face of a steadily increasing population (The total of annual receptions in 2001-2002 was, for example up 1,700 from the previous year). Reasons behind this reduction in loss of life, include the gradual effects of adopting a policy of inclusion, rather than exclusion, for potentially suicidal prisoners, better awareness training for officers, a commendable increase in the number of psychiatrically trained nurses, the use of experienced prisoners as 'listeners' and better drug withdrawal treatment. The introduction of in cell TV in much the same period (and a useful 'baby sitter') may also have

played a part. In addition, despite an increasingly ageing prison population, the overall mortality rate has also been reducing. It would appear,
however, that the rate of serious assaults on prisoners has been on the
increase though the same does not apply to staff (methods of recording
have also been changing). Nevertheless, despite some continuing examples
of concerted indiscipline, it would be accurate to say that this aspect is nowhere as worrying as it was ten or twenty years ago. Meantime, whilst there
are problems with nurse recruitment on occasions, the new contractual
arrangements for the provision of medical services seems to be operating
reasonably well. Generally, the harm reduction policies being pursued to
counter public health concerns as a result of illegal drug misuse seem to be
sensible.

Crime Prevention

In January 2004, Scotland's prison population, at a rate of 129 prisoners
per 100,000 of the national population, was one of the highest in the
European Union. This is an unhappy situation, despite Scotland also having
amongst the widest ranges of community-based sentences available and
against an apparent drop in the crime rate during the 1990s. The prime
purpose of incarceration must surely be the protection of the public from
the activities of dangerous or persistent criminals, in which respect, through
secure custody, the SPS provides an appropriate service. However, the time
in prison should also be used to try and encourage reduced future criminal
behaviour, which will require interaction between SPS staff, individual
prisoners, possibly their peers and also their families (so far a hitherto
untapped but hugely influential group). Whilst some results may be achieved
by formal programmes such as addiction and anger management, my
conclusion is that the bulk of changing behaviour might be achieved by a)
the steady example of prison staff as role models and leaders, together with
b) focussed pressure from close relatives (who more than anyone do not
want the prisoner to be released in exactly the same 'bad' old ways). Having
said that, the most important gaps appear to be as follows;

Short-term Prisoners

Little or nothing is being done for these individuals, either because there
are staff shortages (and therefore different priorities), or because there is
so little time available to engage with these prisoners in any meaningful
way. Either this large group should be found community-based punishments
in future (and, therefore, not hamper the work of prison staff with more

serious offenders) or as a minimum each and everyone of them should at least complete a substance misuse programme (especially on how to handle alcohol, which continues to fuel a great deal of crime across Scotland's housing estates and streets).

Young Offenders

If left unchecked, these are tomorrow's adult offenders. Whilst there are small encouraging signs of regime focus at HMP&YOI Polmont, not nearly enough is being done to really tackle offending behaviour head on with all the inmates (and, again, their families). In future, only specially selected and trained staff should be employed at this most critically important institution, which should be led (uninterrupted) by the most charismatic leader that can be found in the SPS.

Women Offenders

Main efforts have hitherto concentrated on safety and decency. Much more sustained effort is now required to give all women offenders a much more meaningful regime which may lead to employment on release. As stated previously, however, the majority of these damaged individuals should not be in prison (everyone from the Scottish Executive agrees, so too even the Judiciary, yet all the indications are that their number in jail will continue to spiral; is anyone in charge out there?).

Other more detailed comments and issues are as follows;

- Needs and Risk Assessments - The SPS now focuses more accurately on this aspect, especially at Edinburgh, Glenochil and until relatively recently, at Peterhead.
- Offending Behaviour Programmes - A much better balance needs to be struck between slavish adherence to KPI's (Key Performance Indicators which are standards set by the Executive but in reality are controlled by 'bean counters') and the actual needs of prisoners.
- Drug and Alcohol Misuse - In 2003/4, a shocking seven out of ten prisoners were found to have serious substance misuse on admission, reflecting an almost out of control situation on some of Scotland's streets (18,186 offenders from 23,508 admissions). The percentage so affected at Cornton Vale is routinely even higher. Whilst a number of excellent initiatives have been introduced by the SPS to tackle this huge and ever-growing problem (such as case workers being recently introduced

from Cranstoun Drug Services to most Scottish prisons), much more could be done to focus on alcohol misuse.

- Work - There is not always enough work, or the appropriate type of work, available in every prison.

- Education - There still needs to be better incentives for prisoners to participate in education programmes, and it must never be forgotten that the prime thrust of prison education must be to concentrate on those who have very poor reading, writing and communication skills.

- Food - Low cost prison food may be failing to provide adequate nutrition and could actually be contributing to poor behaviour . The daily budget for food and drink of £1.57 per prisoner has not been changed since 1996.

- Preparation for Release - At long last, the SPS, having realised how important a process induction is - literally a life saver at some establishments like Greenock where the suicide rate dropped dramatically after its proper introduction - is now turning its attention to much better pre-release arrangements. As I retired as Chief Inspector (or rather, as I was retired as Chief Inspector), it was apparent that HMPs Edinburgh, Greenock and Polmont had really began to get a hold of this vitally important aspect, something other prisons will now hopefully be copying . Essentially this comes down to ensuring that a prisoner on release has the mechanisms in place to get a roof over their head, some control on addictions and the basic means to seek employment, the entire aim being to prevent an otherwise fairly predictable spiral into further imprisonment.

- Management and Staff - The supreme importance of managers and staff as role models to help bring about a sustained reduction in offending behaviour cannot be over emphasised. Yet, a detailed examination of the workings of privately-run establishments reveal some worrying trends. Rightly, the constant focus is on reducing costs (and to make profits for shareholders, which is a slightly different matter!). Nevertheless, low wages and no pensions in private prisons means a high turnover in staff, with new recruits constantly being trained (whereas the hardened criminals on the wings are already trained). This model is constantly held up to the public staff as an example of how to proceed and, is, in my opinion the most insidious threat of all. Privately-run institutions are better at building low cost and modern prison halls, and, in my opinion, for focussing on remands or similar groups not requiring role models to bring about 'rehabilitation', whereas serious sex offenders and the like should be dealt with by public servants, and plenty of them! This is not, however, the thrust of fellow civil servants in the Scottish Executive. It is here that there must be strict control, if our prisons are not in future, once more to become 'human zoos'. And this despite all the fine words about' rehabilitation'.

Final Comment

In recent years, there have been tantalising glimpses of a prison service in Scotland that could help bring about a sustained reduction in serious crime. This must be the renewed thrust in future. The results that the public are entitled to may only be achieved if there are far fewer petty criminals incarcerated, and, - if the 'bean counters' are kept at bay! Some latter day John Howard or Elizabeth Frye penal reformers are still sorely needed, both within and without the SPS.

Chapter 10

Civil Justice and Legal Aid

Mike Dailly

Why do we need a civil justice system? As the former Lord Chief Justice suggests 'A system of civil justice is essential to the maintenance of a civilised society. The law itself provides the basic structure within which commerce and industry operate. It safeguards the rights of individuals, regulates their dealing with others and enforces the duties of government' (Woolf 1995). While the need for a mechanism to determine disputes is perhaps uncontroversial, the question of who benefits from it is not. If a citizen cannot properly engage in a legal process, he or she may have little or no chance of success (see, for example, Samuel 1988). That is particularly so in the United Kingdom which relies upon an adversarial system of justice where each party must present their own case in order to win. Those with deep pockets have, on the face of it, a big advantage. Wealthy litigants can employ the best legal representation money can buy - they can pay for the most impressive experts to give evidence on their behalf. Their case can be presented as powerfully as possible.

Civil justice will only be fair then if both parties have 'equality of arms'. There can be no equal access to justice unless poor litigants can present their case as reasonably well as wealthy opponents. In the UK, the principle of 'equality of arms' is safeguarded by Article 6 *of the Human Rights Act 1998* (see three cases below). This principle is not absolute, and the state may choose to place legitimate restrictions on the availability of free legal representation. Restrictions may be based on, for example, the seriousness of the matter, the applicant's financial circumstances and the prospects of success (OSJI 2005).

Legal Aid in Scotland

In Scotland, the Scottish Executive meets its Article 6 obligations through a legal aid scheme administered by the Scottish Legal Aid Board (SLAB). SLAB will fund civil litigation where an applicant's annual 'disposable income' does not exceed £9,570, and their capital does not exceed £10,779. These limits are effective from April 2005 and are generally uprated annually (see further slab.org.uk/profession/mailshots/2005/leaflet6_april2005.pdf). Applicants must also demonstrate to SLAB that their case has 'probable cause', i.e., reasonable prospects of success, and that it is reasonable in all the circumstances that civil legal be granted. Where an applicant's disposable income is below £2,931 and their capital is below £6,465, they will receive free legal aid. Where their income or capital is over these sums they must pay a contribution, which is generally one third of disposable income over the £2,931 limit.

Median household income in Scotland for the year 2003/04 was £17,472 (DWP 2005). It is, therefore, apparent that most working people in Scotland are either financially ineligible for civil legal aid or are only eligible if they pay a large financial contribution. In 1994, there were 23,750 grants of civil legal aid, with that number falling to 12,332 in 2004. Likewise net spending on civil legal aid fell from £25.6m in 1997 to £18.6m in 2004. Civil legal aid is becoming increasingly irrelevant to those in low or modestly paid work.

This is perhaps why the Scottish Executive has recently announced it is considering increasing the upper financial limits for eligibility (BBC *Newsonline* 17 June 2005, news.bbc.co.uk/1/hi/scotland/4104598.stm). There can be little doubt that unless eligibility limits for civil legal aid are dramatically improved, legal aid will become the preserve of the poor and low paid couples going through separation, divorce or custody disputes. If ordinary people cannot access the civil courts for want of money, the system is clearly not working. But, of course, we have known this for more than 25 years.

Accessing Justice

In 1980, the *Hughes Commission* (1980: paragraph 14.2.) reported that the civil justice system was 'unduly cumbersome, slow, and costly ... for these and other reasons, such as excessive formality, persons wishing to assert or defend their rights are sometimes unwilling or are financially unable to resort to the civil courts in Scotland'. There have since been many further calls for a comprehensive civil justice review (see, for example, IDRWG 2000, SCC 2005). However, to date reform has been piecemeal and disjointed. Recently, the Scottish Executive acknowledged that the civil justice system had to be, in the words of Minister for Justice, Cathy Jamieson MSP, at the Annual Dinner of the Scottish Branch of the Chartered Institute of Arbitrators (14 March 2005) 'fit for its purpose in the 21st century – modern, accessible and efficient'. At present, it is not.

Unfortunately, recent procedural reforms have been far from 'accessible and efficient'. To take two examples. Firstly, the Scottish Executive has invested millions of pounds in its 'Debt Arrangement Scheme' to make it easier for debtors to repay multiple debts. But the Scheme can only be accessed through 'accredited money advisors'. In 2005, after the first year of operation, only 29 money advisors were accredited and take up was negligible (moneyscotland.gov.uk, see also the *Debt Arrangement & Attachment (Scotland) Act 2002*). The Scheme relies upon a sizeable amount of form filling and is procedurally complex. Essentially, it has little more power than a 'time to pay' application – which in contrast can be completed by any individual on an A4 sheet of paper, in minutes. Secondly, the *Housing (Scotland) Act 2006* created a new Private Rented Housing Panel to provide tenants with a quick, cheap and straightforward remedy to get repairs done. The law in Scotland has generally been unable to force landlords to implement important repair obligations. So the Scottish Executive came up with a potential solution which it has restricted to the private rented sector. Why? This represents about 6 per cent of all households in Scotland. Why not extend it to another 27 per cent of households by including the social rented sector?

Justice Denied Through Disproportionate Costs

We need to get back to the basic principles identified by the Hughes Commission over 25 years ago. Our system of civil justice should be easy to access, fair, and speedy. Reforms should tested against these fundamental principles. Some progress has been made on speed. The average waiting time in the sheriff court for ordinary cause actions is now 11 weeks – 1 week faster than the courts own target of 12 weeks. In the Court of Session, it takes on average 34 weeks to obtain a proof – the target is 19 weeks, so there remains room for improvement (SCS 2005). But of more concern is cost. Cost becomes an acute problem if a litigant has to risk more on potential legal expenses than the sum sued for or opposed. For example, if a litigant has a breach of contract claim for £2,000 and the matter proceeds to proof at the sheriff court, the pursuer may be looking at over £6,000 in expenses in the event of failure. On the ordinary cause scale – this would include the cost of the litigant's own solicitors fees, the cost of the opponent's 'judicial expenses', and various outlays including shorthand writers fees, based upon one day of proof. The sum could be much more if the case required several days of evidence, or was delayed or continued. Why would anyone assume this risk? Of course, risk works both ways – would a defender really risk losing £8,000, or would they rather settle the case for £1,500 plus expenses?

   If in many cases it is uneconomic for citizens to access the civil courts, then justice is being denied. Interestingly, in our example, if the litigant was suing for £50,000 and the case proceeded to proof the risk of expenses would not increase. Accessing the sheriff court ordinary cause procedure will always cost a certain amount of money regardless of the value of the case.

A problem occurs when that cost is out of proportion with what is being claimed or defended. One suggestion to resolve this difficulty has been to extend the sheriff court small claims procedure limit to £5,000. John Home Robertson MSP and the Scottish Consumer Council have been among the most vociferous advocates for increasing the small claims limit to £5,000, while many lawyers, including myself, and the trade union movement have been opposed to any increase (Dailly 2004:28). In England and Wales, the small claims limit has been raised twice – to £3,000 in 1996 and to £5,000 in 1999. In Scotland, the limit remains at £750. Empirical evidence has confirmed that increases in England and Wales have only produced a minor uptake in claims. More importantly, research has concluded that 'the majority of small claims cases with a value between £3,000 and £5,000 involve commercial organisations suing other organisations' (Baldwin 2002). All of the evidence reveals that the small claims procedure has been a bit of a flop from a 'consumer' perspective. Recent research by the Scottish Consumer Council (2003) confirmed that only 7 per cent of members of the public surveyed would consider using the small claims procedure for a consumer problem. The small claims procedure is fine for commercial debt collectors but is unpopular with ordinary citizens. Extending a scheme that has a narrow take up makes no sense as a means to open up access to the civil justice system.

There are other difficulties with the small claims procedure. Firstly, the current small claims system is inappropriate for any case where an expert witness is needed. How do you establish that a car was unfit for the purpose for which it was intended or that a plasma screen television had a latent defect? In any case, where expert evidence is essential the small claims procedure will always be inappropriate because the successful litigant can only recover £75 in expenses (see Note 1). Who will pay for the expert witness fee? Again, claims may become uneconomic. Secondly, despite being designed to be an informal procedure (which it is not), a small claims action is adversarial in nature. No free legal representation is available because civil legal aid is excluded from the scheme. The scheme's virtue – 'you don't need representation' - is its downfall for many citizens. Around 800,000 adults in Scotland have very low adult literacy and numeracy skills (Scottish Executive 2001). While a well educated professional may find it manageable to present their own small claim, a person who finds it difficult to read and write may not. Such people could be at a major disadvantage without the benefit of representation. But representation costs money, and loading extra costs onto modest claims for money brings us full circle to disproportionate cost. In other words, if the cost of raising an action exceeds the sum sued for the process will not be 'easy to access'. So what are the alternatives?

Feasible Alternatives and a New Civil Tribunal

We could take all 'non-contentious' payment actions out of the sheriff court. This could include any claim for money up to £25,000 where the debtor did not proceed with a legal defence - the figure of £25,000 would be consistent with the *Debtors (Scotland) Act 1987* and the *Consumer Credit Act 1974*, which both extend to debts with a value up to £25,000. In terms of administrative efficiency, actions would still be raised in the sheriff court but where no legal defence or response was intimated by the defender, the case could be automatically remitted to a new 'civil tribunal'. Payment actions excluded from the civil tribunal would include actions for recovery or possession of heritable property, personal injury claims and housing disrepair cases. The reason for these exclusions is because such actions are either complex, contentious or particularly suited to the sheriff court because of the need for hearings on evidence or legal argument.

The Scottish Courts Administration estimated that 90 per cent of payment claims in the sheriff court were for less than £5,000 in 1998. We also know that in the majority of sheriff court cases decree for payment passes on an undefended basis. In 2002, this was the position in 75 per cent of ordinary cause actions, 98 per cent of summary cause actions, and 54 per cent of small claims (Scottish Executive 2002b). Accordingly, in the bulk of payment actions the question in dispute is essentially how quickly and over what period of time can the debt be repaid? Tribunals hearing debt actions where the level of repayment was in dispute could be chaired by a legally qualified chairperson and two lay-members, one person from a banking or credit industry background and another from a social work or welfare rights background.

The tribunal could be empowered to consider and deal with all of the debtor's debts, and to provide a long lasting and holistic approach to their financial problems. It could appoint a free money advisor or law centre solicitor to assist in this process, for the Scottish Executive and Scottish local authorities already publicly fund a large number of advisors (of varying levels of skill and experience) to provide free money advice, as well as law centre solicitors to assist in more complex cases involving debt and diligence. For debt cases generally, a new civil tribunal could replace the poorly conceived 'Debt Arrangement Scheme'. Unlike 'Debt Arrangement Scheme', the tribunal could be empowered to freeze or lower excessive contractual rates of interest running on debts. It could abate excessive administrative or penalty charges added on to debts. In this regard, *Which?* magazine has estimated that UK banks generate £3 billion pounds pa in consumer bank charges (see news.bbc.co.uk/1/hi/business/3621002.stm) and excessive bank charges compound and exacerbate indebtedness unnecessarily (see further, Govan Law Centre's site on this subject at bankcharges.info). A new civil tribunal could also restrict legal expenses to a modest and affordable sum. This could give more debtors the possibility of repaying debts as opposed to the sledgehammer of bankruptcy or forced poverty.

A civil tribunal could hear 'contentious' payment actions, that is defended money actions (with the same exclusions as discussed earlier) up to the value of £5,000. This could replace the small claims procedure in the sheriff court. Significantly, a new civil tribunal could be inquisitorial in nature so as to obviate the need for formal representation and reduce the cost of dispute resolution. An inquisitorial tribunal is charged with determining the facts of a case, whereas an adversarial system acts as an impartial referee between the parties. Indeed, some civil law countries have traditionally embraced an inquisitorial or interventionist system in their criminal or administrative courts (Jolowicz 2003). If tribunal applicants wanted to be represented then it would be an irrecoverable expense, win or lose. For the tribunal to be easily accessible no party expenses should be payable except in special circumstances. In this regard, a rule similar to Employment Tribunal procedure could be adopted whereby a party's legal expenses are only payable where a case is misconceived or where a litigant has been vexatious, and the Tribunal thinks it reasonable to make an award. Representation would be unnecessary because the tribunal would be charged with the task of assisting both parties to achieve a just and fair outcome. It would be the tribunal's role to decide what witnesses should be called. The tribunal would examine witnesses, while providing parties with an opportunity to ask additional questions. There would no recording of evidence by short-hand writers to keep the cost of proceedings proportionate to their value and importance.

The problem of expert testimony in consumer disputes before the tribunal could be resolved by a 'remit to a person of skill' procedure (ordinary cause rule 29.2 provides for a 'remit to a person of skill' procedure, see: scotcourts.gov.uk/library/rules/ordinarycause/ocr.pdf). Where the tribunal required expert evidence, it could appoint an independent expert to produce a report and, if necessary, give testimony. The expert's report could be given a legal presumption of being conclusive (subject to rebuttal on cause shown). This would provide an expeditious mechanism for parties to resolve technical consumer disputes. The cost of expert evidence would be payable by the losing party, in additional to a small nominal fee to the tribunal for its time. This would open up access to justice for the many, not the few. Any citizen with a payment or consumer dispute would be able to access the civil tribunal without fear of cost. Dissatisfied parties would have the right of appeal to the Sheriff Principal on a point of law only. A summary of how this proposed system would fit with the existing civil court system is set on the next page.

Conclusion

A civil tribunal system for Scotland would be both radical and progressive. While not providing the same degree of expertise and thoroughness as an evidential hearing presided over by a sheriff, it could provide the basis of a high quality dispute resolution mechanism. It would be impartial, robust and fair. Its cost would be proportionate to the level of claims before it in terms of financial value and importance. Most importantly, it could provide easy, fair and speedy access to civil justice for all citizens in Scotland.

Cases

- Airey v. Ireland (1979) 2 EHRR 305
- Golder v. UK (1975) 1 EHRR 524.
- Steel and Morris v. UK Case No.68416/01. 15 February 2005

Note

(1) This is the general rule. No expenses can be awarded where the value of the claim is less than £200. The £75 limit does not apply where the defender has not stated a defence, or having stated a defence, has not proceeded with it, or having stated and proceeded with a defence has not acted in good faith as to its merits. It does not apply where there has been unreasonable conduct by either party, or in relation to an appeal: see further *Sheriff Courts (Scotland) Act 1971*, section 36B(3), and the *Act of Sederunt (Small Claim Rules) 2002*, rule 26.

A Proposed Civil Tribunal System

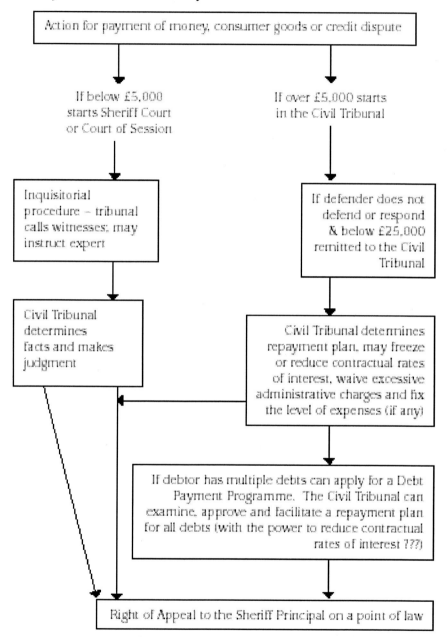

Action for payment of money, consumer goods or credit dispute

If below £5,000 starts Sheriff Court or Court of Session

If over £5,000 starts in the Civil Tribunal

Inquisitorial procedure – tribunal calls witnesses; may instruct expert

If defender does not defend or respond & below £25,000 remitted to the Civil Tribunal

Civil Tribunal determines facts and makes judgment

Civil Tribunal determines repayment plan, may freeze or reduce contractual rates of interest, waive excessive administrative charges and fix the level of expenses (if any)

If debtor has multiple debts can apply for a Debt Payment Programme. The Civil Tribunal can examine, approve and facilitate a repayment plan for all debts (with the power to reduce contractual rates of interest ???)

Right of Appeal to the Sheriff Principal on a point of law

Chapter 11

Workplace Justice – the oft forgotten arena

Ian Tasker

'Justice' is most often viewed as being to do with communities, courts and criminals. Seldom is justice seen as being about what happens to people in their workplaces and in their working lives. Somehow it is marked off from these others concerns, probably the legacy of employer's ability to run their operations as private concerns and reinforced by limited health and safety legislation. It was hoped by many this situation of insufficient attention given to issues of workplace governance and justice could be changed with the return to office of the Labour Party in 1997. But since 2000, three years after the incoming Labour Government first promised to introduce corporate killing legislation, 117 workers in Scotland have been killed in work-related accidents. In addition, 35 self-employed and 48 members of the public have lost their lives in incidents investigated by the Health and Safety Executive (2004a, 2005a). If we then look at incidents that resulted in injury to workers for the same period, 2000/05, 14,413 suffered major injuries at work and a staggering 52,678 sustained an injury that resulted in three days or more off work (HSE 2004a, 2005a).

While these figures are bad enough, it needs to be remembered that Scotland now has the lowest rate levels of reporting. According to the Labour Force Survey, only 40 per cent of workplace accidents are reported in Scotland against a national figure of 48 per cent and 58 per cent in Wales (HSE 2005a). We should also remember that Scotland witnessed the most appalling tragedy in 1988 when 167 people lost their lives in the Piper Alpha disaster and not a single charge was brought against the company or any individual with management responsibility; this was despite Lord Cullen heavily criticising safety procedures on the rig. More recently, nine workers lost their lives in an incident at the ICL/Stockline plant in Glasgow, the investigation of which is still ongoing. If we also consider the thousands of workers who have lost their lives as a result of negligent exposure to asbestos by their employers, those who have died of other industrial diseases and an, as yet unidentifiable number of work related road deaths, our record in work related deaths is at best unenviable and we would contend a national disgrace. Despite this appalling record not one corporation or single individual has been convicted of culpable homicide following any deaths caused by their own negligence or omissions. This is why we need not only new legislation, but effective legislation. There would have been a public outcry, and rightly so, if so many cases had not been prosecuted following any involuntary death in any other part of our society, but this does not happen in relation to work related deaths.

Table 1: Work-based Injuries and Fatalities in Scotland and Britain

Scotland		2000/01	2001/02	2002/03	2003/04	2004/05
Fatal	Employee	25	24	26	9	33
	Self-employed	12	4	10	6	3
	Member of Public	8	7	10	11	12
Major	Employee	2758	2792	2759	2875	2861
	Self-employed	40	77	87	83	97
Over three days	Employee	11135	10787	10330	10504	9911
	Self-employed	30	70	66	37	46
Great Britain		2000/01	2001/02	2002/03	2003/04	2004/05
Fatal	Employee	202	195	175	156	162
	Self-employed	79	45	44	68	50
	Member of Public	114	88	93	96	85
Major	Employee	270 72	27598	27700	30290	29760
	Self-employed	630	1929	1079	1283	1246
Over three days	Employee	131003	127457	125967	128958	118339
	Self-employed	715	917	951	1114	1132

Source: HSE (various).

Scotland's health and safety record first came under scrutiny in 1999 when Woolfson and Beck (1999) ignited the debate on workplace injuries and for the first time raised concerns that the risks of Scottish workers suffering fatal or major injuries was significantly higher than for workers in other parts of Britain. Woolfson and Beck, using data provided by the Health and Safety Executive, estimated that the risk of suffering a fatal workplace injury in Scotland was twice that of the England and Wales, with the risk of a Scottish worker suffering a serious injury being 26 per cent more likely. The purpose of their paper, in addition to highlighting the anomaly, was to provoke discussion by raising relevant points that required further discussion. The authors suggested investigating the level of management failure on a case-by-case basis to ascertain if Scottish employers were more inclined to cut corners on health and safety management. Another issue out put forward that might explain the discrepancies related to lower levels of deterrents in Scotland, less enforcement by the Health and Safety Executive and Local Authority Environmental Health Officers, lower levels of prosecution and lower penalties imposed by the Courts.

Finally, the authors suggested that continuing budgetary cuts suffered by the HSE and local authority regulators in addition to a move to a more business friendly enforcement philosophy may be having an impact of direct contacts between regulators and workplaces.

Interestingly, following the publication of this paper, Cathy Jamieson (2000) MSP and now Scottish Executive Justice Minister said that it was important to ensure that the Scottish Parliament 'considers and comments on Scottish concerns over issues which other bodies, such as Westminster and the EU, have legislative powers'. At the same time, the MSP lodged a motion calling a Scottish Parliament Standing Commission to be convened to investigate the report. This was rejected. It is right that the Scottish Parliament should be able to consider any matter that impacts on the welfare of Scottish people and it is inevitable that there will be areas of cross over between reserved and devolved powers. The Executive in rejecting the proposal Cathy Jamieson suggested quite clearly body-swerved the issue on the grounds health and safety was a reserved matter.

There appears to have been no consideration given to the impact these tragedies have on those who lose loved ones and suffer major injuries, their fight for justice and compensation and the detrimental effect poor health and safety management has on Scottish enterprises. Ironically, the figures quoted by the authors for fatalities and major injuries for 1996/97 and 1997/98 show an alarming rise in the next seven years when compared to the most recent available data as the Table 2 shows.

All in all, since Woolfson and Beck first published their report there appears to have been little progress made in reducing fatalities and major injuries within Scottish workplaces. The discussion points they advanced are still relevant, providing a suitable base line when considering how we improve our health and safety record.

Table 2: Injuries and Fatalities in Scotland

Type/Year	1996/97	1997/98	2004/05
Fatal Injuries	28	27	36
Major Injuries	2010	2377	2861

Source: HSE.

There is no simple answer as to how we achieve a sustained improvement in protecting workers, but Bill Callaghan, Chair of the Health and Safety Commission, says in his introduction to latest Health and Safety Commission strategy, 'their [HSC] vision is to see health and safety as a cornerstone of a civilised society and, with that, achieve a record of workplace health and safety that leads the world' (HSE 2004b). It would appear that from the statistics above we have a long way to go before we can make such a claim with any degree of honesty and, in any examination of Scotland's record, the STUC believes we have to consider a) corporate homicide, b) the strategic direction of regulators, c) enforcement, regulation and deterrents, d) improved worker involvement in workplace health and safety, and e) occupational health provision in Scotland.

Opportunities for Health and Safety Regime Change in Scotland

Corporate Homicide

Early last year, the Home Office published the *Draft Corporate Manslaughter Bill for England and Wales* that, in theory, would ensure corporations could be brought to book for acts of gross negligence that resulted in deaths of workers or members of the public. While this Draft Bill received a cautious welcome south of the border, it only allows for corporations to be charged, not individuals. This was hardly a surprise as both Jack Straw and David Blunkett had previously made it clear; culpability of individual directors was not on the agenda. To make matters worse, the Draft Bill retained an element of the identification or controlling mind principle, the very issue that has made it virtually impossible to prosecute large corporations in the past.

In order to obtain a prosecution, it would be necessary to identify failings of a 'senior manager'. To the STUC, this would simply allow large unscrupulous organisations to delegate health and safety responsibility to non-senior manager levels. Even the impact assessment attached to the Draft Bill outlined this long awaited legislation would only result in an additional five prosecutions per year, hardly a significant rise when compared to the near three hundred workers that lose their lives each year.

Thankfully, Scotland has its own criminal justice system and the STUC welcomed the decision of the Scottish Executive Justice Minister, Cathy Jamieson, to appoint an Expert Group charged with making recommendations for proposed Corporate Culpable Homicide legislation for Scotland. Equally, we welcomed the Minister's reassurances that, while alignment of the two pieces of legislation would be beneficial, there was no intention of using the Sewell Motion procedure to transpose the Westminster legislation to Holyrood unless that was the express view of the Expert Group. Needless to say for the reasons outlined earlier, the STUC and our nominees on the group, along with a majority of other members, did not support such a move.

In December 2005, the Scottish Executive (2005) published the full recommendations of the Expert Group. The STUC described these proposals as radical and forward thinking. The business community clearly thinks otherwise, and notwithstanding they had a similar number of representatives on the group, they are now describing the proposals as draconian and the report not reflecting the views of certain representative organisation. Even at this stage, they have launched into the usual diatribe about chasing business away from Scotland, lack of inward investment and a witchhunt against directors. All of these allegations are totally unsubstantiated and have not been witnessed in Canada or Australia when similar legislation has been introduced. So why have the recommendations got the business community in Scotland in a such lather, and are their assertions regarding our proposals in any way correct?

It was clear in the early days of the process that the majority of the Expert Group considered the Draft Manslaughter Bill would lead, if unamended, to a piece of ineffective legislation. However, it certainly provided the STUC nominees with a document we could dissect and suggest improvements to and which that we believe will provide the basis for legislation that will protect Scottish workers and reduce the amounts of workplace deaths. What are the Scottish proposals?

In Scotland, our basis of culpability is recklessness, focusing on what the employer knew or ought to have known, as opposed to the stricter test of gross negligence in England and Wales. The Expert Group has also recommended that the level of management failure should not be restricted to 'senior management' and should extend to management at any appropriate level which more accurately reflects the way employing organisations operate. The Scottish proposals are also suggesting shifting the onus of proof once the primary breach is established. This would mean that companies will have to present evidence to establish lack of recklessness on their part if they are to escape conviction. The majority of the Expert Group also advocated the establishment of an individual director's offence, ensuring that directors who fail meet their legal obligations under the *Health and Safety at Work Act* 1974 at the expense of other considerations (such as directors' bonuses, profit sharing or increasing dividends to shareholders) are held accountable in the event of a fatality. It is said that the existing common law offence of culpable homicide allows for this, but no director of a employing organization in Scotland has ever been charged with, let alone found guilty of, culpable homicide following the death of a worker. In addition to that offence, the recommendations of the Expert Group suggest a stand alone offence to ensure that individual directors and/or managers who are found to have made a significant contribution to a death can be prosecuted.

The Expert Group also agreed that any Scottish legislation should cover all employers and not simply corporate bodies as is the case under the Westminster proposals. It would appear ludicrous that non-incorporated bodies such as friendly societies and clubs should be immune from prosecution and Scottish legislation should be consistent across all employer organizations including Crown agencies. It is also envisaged that any new legislation should apply to offences committed by all Scottish companies irrespective of where they operate at home or abroad. This is vitally important; not least to ensure that oil companies operating outwith territorial waters are included within the legislation. Finally, the Group has put forward a wide range of innovative sanctions to be made available to the courts including equity fines hitting the shareholders' pockets not the consumer, corporate probation, community service, health and safety administration and imprisonment of individuals.

From this, it may be said that our proposals will result in far stricter legislation, and why not if it is right for Scotland? However, the business community is being economical with the truth when they make their loaded comparisons with the Draft Corporate Manslaughter Bill. They are failing to mention that the Draft Bill has been subject to scrutiny by a Joint Home Affairs Select and Department of Work and Pensions Select Committee (JHA/DWP 2006). This Committee, which reported in December, has made a number of recommendations that if carried would result in fairly similar legislation in the two jurisdictions. They have suggested: a) amending the Bill to ensure individual directors can be prosecuted, b) extension of the Crown Immunity provision to cover more Crown bodies including the army when not in the field of combat, c) changing the ambiguous senior management identification test to one of management failure, d) extending the jurisdiction of the offence to cover deaths in other parts of the United

Kingdom, with a view to further extending the jurisdiction to cover deaths in other European countries in the future, and d) a wider range of innovative sanctions against companies.

The Committees state in their final report that the Government should be doing all it can to ensure that there is as little variation as possible between Scotland, England and Wales, going on to say that the recommendations contained in their joint report would bring the Government's Draft Bill closer to the reforms proposed by the Scottish Expert Group. This is an endorsement of the view of the majority of the Expert Group that we should not align with the poorest and least effective legislation but that the Westminster Government should align with our recommendations.

HSE/HSC Strategic Direction

In 2000, the Government realised an emerging problem in that the rate of workplace deaths and major accidents had reached a (high) plateau and in some cases were showing an increase. The Government decided to throw down a challenge to employers and set a number of challenging targets to be met over a ten year period, namely: to reduce the number of working days lost by 30 per cent, reduce fatal and major injuries by 10 per cent, and reduce the incidences of occupational ill health by 20 per cent. (An interim target was set for 50 per cent of the overall reduction to have been achieved by 2005.) Quite clearly we have passed the stage where half of the overall target should have been met but the HSE's own view is pessimistic to say the least.

It says that for each target: a) the number of working days lost has fallen, and the 15 per cent target has possibly been met, b) incidences of occupational ill-health have fallen, and the 10 per cent target has possibly been achieved, and c) on reducing fatal and major injuries that 'no discernible trend [has been identified] that this has been changed'. In respect of this last point, with a glance back at the tables at the beginning of this chapter, it could be argued that the figures for Scotland are actually getting worse.

Trade unions and safety campaigners were not alone in expressing concern that the HSE had little realistic chance of delivering on these targets. In July 2004, another Department of Work and Pensions Select Committee produced a report on the work of the Health and Safety Commission and Executive (HCW and PC 2004). The Committee's report raised a number of concerns and made a number of recommendations including;

i)   The endorsement of the union Prospect's view that the number of inspectors in HSE's Field Operation Directorate should be doubled, and that substantial resources were required between 2005 and 2008;

ii)   Supporting the view of the trade union movement that inspection, backed up by enforcement, is the most effective method of encouraging employers to meet their legal obligation under health and safety legislation;

iii) Raising concern at the low level of accident investigation and proactive inspection and recommending that resources be made available to address this;

iv)   The requirement for evidence-based analysis before adopting a policy of 'earned autonomy' form of inspection for employers demonstrating established good practice. The Committee was concerned that 'improper pressures' could be placed on workers to achieve a reduction in accident rates;

v)   An increased role for trade union health and safety representatives, including the right to issue improvement and prohibition notices;

vi)   The Government should deliver on all its outstanding legislative commitments outlined in the Revitalising Health and Safety Strategy document, including increased penalties and specific legal duties to placed on directors to protect their workers health and safety;

vii) Expressed disappointment at the lack of progress made towards the creation of a national occupational health service, with the recommendation of increased resources in order to ensure the HSE meets the 2010 target for occupational health.

These are only six of the 35 recommendations the committee made in order to ensure the HSE was adequately equipped to get the revitalising strategy back on track. The Government totally ignored the report of this committee and continues happily along the road of deregulation and appeasement of employers with little respect for those on the shopfloor.

If we needed any evidence that the HSE was embracing the new regulatory enforcement framework put forward by the Hampton review and publicly supported by the Chancellor of the Exchequer, we need look no further than the latest HSE strategy document (HSE 2004b:10). In this, the HSE states that it and local authorities will not intervene proactively where the proper management of risks can be assured following the Chancellor's de-regulation mantra that 'there is no inspection without justification'. There is widespread alarm among trade unions, safety campaigners and the general public that, at a time when the statistics indicate the need for an enforcement based on efficient inspection and enforcement, the Government and the Health and Safety Commission think they know better.

Enforcement, Regulation and Deterrents

There can be little doubt that enforcement activity by HSE inspectors and local authority officials is diminishing and only partly due to strategic direction. This is also attributable to real-time cuts in budgets for the HSE and competing priorities for local authorities' environmental health departments such as food standards, noise pollution and, in Scotland enforcing the smoking ban in public places. Throughout the United Kingdom, the numbers of employers charged and convicted of health and safety offences between 2004/04 and 2004/05 has fallen substantially. In Scotland, for the year 2003/04, 268 charges were brought and 110 convictions secured. For the following year, records show that only 140 charges were brought (- 48 per cent) resulting in 75 convictions (-32 per cent).

In a statement, available on the HSE website, Justin McCracken said, 'We know that we are devoting about the same amount of resource, year-on-year, to investigation and enforcement activities but producing fewer prosecutions' (HSE 2005b). The HSE then go on to justify lower levels on enforcement on external pressures such as the 'work related deaths protocol' that commits the HSE to working jointly with the Police to investigate any workplace death in England and Wales. There is currently no such arrangement in Scotland, although we would have to accept that the ongoing investigation into the ICL/Stockline tragedy and the protracted legal case following the Larkhall Gas explosion, that attracted a record fine of £16 million, have to have had an adverse impact on HSE resources in Scotland and their ability to sustain enforcement activity. What has to be concerning for Scotland is that McCracken's statement quite clearly appears to focus on matters affecting the HSE in England and Wales, referring to the joint investigation protocol, the Crown Prosecution Service and Magistrates Courts.

Workers in the United Kingdom should not rely on the Health and Safety Commission to bring forward new legislation to increase the protection afforded within the workplace - this would quite clearly be against the Government's de-regulation agenda. We only have to look at the legislative commitments contained in the action points of the Revitalising Health and Safety Strategy published in 2000 to have an indication of the Government's lack of commitment to legislate on health and safety:

- Action point 7 –to extend the £20,000 maximum fine in lower courts to a wider range of offences with power to imprison for most offences.
- Action point 9 – to consider more innovative penalties for health and safety offences.
- Action point 11 – placing statutory health and safety duties on directors.

- Action point 15 – to remove Crown Immunity from health and safety enforcement, leaving Crown employers open to prosecution in a similar manner to any other employer.
- Action point 16 – amend the 1974 Act to reflect the changing world of work to ensure all workers irrespective of employment status are afforded the same protection.

To date, the Government has failed to find the parliamentary time or perhaps, indeed, the political will to take any of these issues forward despite the recommendation of the DWP Select Committee that they should do so as soon as possible. Leaving aside the Government's failure to legislate, there quite clearly needs to be a review of sentencing in respect of health and safety convictions. For 2004/05, the average fines for successful cases taken by the HSE and for 2003/04 for those taken by local authorities were £9,383 and £3,952 respectively. These figures are, we would suggest, likely to be distorted by a number of larger fines and may therefore not be an accurate reflection on the fuller picture. However, if we consider that the upper limit for financial sanction following a conviction is £20,000 or a period of imprisonment then it could be argued that the penalties being imposed by Scottish Courts are not acting as a deterrent.

Improved worker involvement in health and safety

The introduction of the *Safety Representatives and Safety Committees Regulations* in 1977 provided trade unions with the framework to develop workplace health and safety and their success in rising to this challenge was reflected in massive reduction in workplace deaths and fatal injuries in the years following their introduction. Prior to the introduction of the *Health and Safety at Work Act 1974*, it had become clear from the early part of the twentieth century that in the absence of legislation, there is little chance of employers setting up joint consultation procedures. Trade unions accepted the challenge with relish and an HSE survey of workplaces one year after the implementation in 1980 found that 79 per cent of employees surveyed were employed on workplaces where there was a trade union appointed health and safety representative. It is estimated that there are currently around 200,000 health and safety representatives in the United Kingdom with many trade unions embarking on campaign to recruit more during 2006. There have been numerous studies that indicate that you are less likely to suffer injury or occupational ill-health if you work in a unionised workplace than elsewhere. However, the positive effect of trade unions is not restricted to Britain – indeed, in many other countries the structures and powers provided to representatives are far wider reaching than in Britain, extending to roving safety representatives in Australia and Sweden, the right to stop dangerous work in Sweden and the right for Australian Health and Safety representatives to issue provisional improvement notices.

Over twenty-five years have passed since the introduction of the safety representatives regulations and trade unions believe the time is right to provide improved rights and, most importantly, increased employment protection for health and safety representatives. In many industries, such as offshore oil and construction, being a trade union appointed health and safety representative comes at a price and often this involves the loss of their job, which is unacceptable. While this is clearly a reserved matter to Westminster, the Scottish Executive should be promoting healthier and safer workplaces and the benefits these bring to business and the economy. There is an opportunity for the Executive to utilise some of the trade union resources to develop worker involvement in non-unionised workplaces. The STUC is currently working with a small number of voluntary sector organisations with HSE funding, all of which have made significant improvements in joint participation in a short space of time. Most of these organisations receive some level of public funding and the STUC believes that Scottish voluntary sector organisations who wish to develop worker involvement in health and safety should be allowed to factor the cost into funding bids.

Occupational Health and Rehabilitation

Currently in Scotland, only 20 per cent of the workforce have access to effective occupational health services, including rehabilitation through their work. The STUC believes that effective services involve identification and monitoring of hazards, risk management, providing occupational health and safety information and training to workers and monitoring trends in health. Trade union representatives play an important role in many aspects of occupational health provision but the figures for major injuries and more than three day absences and other incidences of work related ill-health suggests that far more needs to be done to ensure occupational ill-health in Scotland receives the same attention as other health matters. There is a marked difference to the provision of occupational health support between the private and public sectors with many private sector companies, and even some local authorities, contracting their services out to private health providers. These kind of services are generally not accessible to workers until such time as they have had an extended illness, facing a cut in sick pay arrangements or dismissal. It is still far too easy for employers to dismiss workers on the grounds of capability and, understandably, this along with proper and equitable occupational health advisors makes workers extremely suspicious of the employers motives when asking workers to undergo medical examinations. While many workers in trade unions have far better protection than others, both with regard to safety and occupational health, the delivery of health interventions has deteriorated since the days when industries ran their own rehabilitation and convalescent centres.

Conclusion

The STUC believes we are at a turning point in relation to our campaign to secure corporate homicide legislation. However, trade unions and others have to continue to lobby the Scottish Executive Justice Department and all other Parliamentary parties to ensure we secure the right legislation for Scotland as outlined earlier. We all have to ensure that pressure is not placed on the Scottish Executive to tow the Westminster line and we believe to do so would be a sad reflection on the powers of our Scottish Parliament. In the coming period, the nonsense that has been spouted by business leaders will be ratcheted up. This will become more intense if the Westminster Government does not revise its draft legislation. The most disappointing thing is that responsible employers and directors have little to fear under the Experts Group's recommendations in the same way that responsible motorists have nothing to fear if the adhere to the rules of the road. However, if you transgress the laws in either case, either by cutting corners for personal or business gain and cause the death of a third party then the outcome should be the same. You should be held to account in either event. This does not happen at the moment in relation to workplace fatalities and this is a grave injustice.

The STUC also believes that if any real improvement is to be made in Scotland's health and safety record then there must be an end to the drift towards de-regulation and the Health and Safety Executive's 'business friendly' enforcement agenda. It will also be necessary for the Westminster Government and the Scottish Executive to examine the resources provided for health and safety enforcement. In the case of the latter, although local authorities, funded by the Executive have responsibility for a growing number of Scottish workplaces, health and safety enforcement has a number of competing priorities, food standards, noise abatement and more recently, smoking legislation to name only a few. We are squeezing enforcement agencies to the bone and are endangering the activities that underpin our health and safety culture, where inspection and enforcement focus the minds of employers and workers. All other activity such as provision of advice, although important, is secondary to the overall aim to achieve safer and healthier workplaces.

While most of the issues in relation to improving worker involvement are of a reserved nature there will shortly be a consultation by the HSE on proposed changes to the *Safety Representatives and Safety Committees Regulations*. While our understanding is that this will not go as far as roving safety representatives, the right to stop dangerous work and to issue provisional improvement notices, we have to ensure that trade unions, safety campaigners and academics are submitting responses calling for these additional provisions. The Scottish Executive through the Scottish Centre for Healthy Working Lives has started to look at occupational health provision mainly to small and medium enterprises. While this is welcome, in comparison to Scandinavian countries not dissimilar in population size to Scotland, we are only scratching the surface and on a tightly controlled budget. We believe the only way to tackle the problem of occupational ill health is to provide a properly funded occupational health service paid for by the state that is accessible to all through the NHS.

From this April, the NHS will be able to recover the costs of treating personal injury cases, including work related injuries when the injured party claims compensation through the courts. These costs amounting to approximately £8 million per annum will go back to individual NHS trust to be spent in any way they want. The STUC believes that the recovery of such costs should have been extended to include treatment of occupational ill-health and disease. This could have generated income to the NHS in Scotland of over £100 million that we argue should be directed towards developing an occupational health system of which we could be proud. The issue of justice and health and safety will always lead to confusion between reserved and devolved issues, but we should not allow either Government to avoid their responsibilities by passing the buck. There have been calls in the past for a Scottish Standing Commission to be convened to examine our health and safety record and to include Scottish politicians in this debate. It may be that now is the time to revisit this option.

Chapter 12

'Can't do the time?' International alternatives to jail

Nick McKerrell

There are many elements of Scottish criminal law and the criminal justice system that are unique and set it apart from other jurisdictions especially English Law. The 1707 Act of Union guaranteed the distinct identity of Scots Law with its own personnel and courts. Criminal law especially retained its identity with the supreme court of England, the House of Lords, having no power to influence it at all. (This is not the case in civil law where the House of Lords is the highest appeal court for Scots law, this being determined soon after the Act of Union.) This is true even in 2006 where Scottish criminal law has different approaches and procedures to the English system. For example, the Scottish criminal courts have a greater reliance on a common law – that is, a judge-made approach – to criminal offences rather than looking to parliamentary statutes. However, there is one area where there is a clear synchronicity with the English system and that is the levels of imprisonment. For a small Northern European country, Scotland has one of the highest rates of imprisonment in the whole of the continent. For every 100,000 people in our country 132 are imprisoned. In Europe, only England and Wales, Spain and Portugal have comparable rates in Western Europe (*World Prison Brief*, February 2004 prisonstudies.org).

Is this inevitable? Well, if countries of similar size are examined there are clear divergences with the Scottish situation. For example Norway, a country with a population of 4.5 million, has an imprisonment rate half that of Scotland: with 65 people jailed for every 100,000. It is the purpose of this chapter to compare what happens in other capitalist legal systems with a view to finding if any positive lessons can be gleaned from them. Linked to this task is the question of why the current situation has developed in Scotland. So in examining the international alternatives to jail, the chapter poses the question 'Could they happen here?' It is clear that the imprisonment issue is not one that will disappear in the immediate future in Scotland. In 2004, around 6,600 people were in Scottish jails. The Scottish Executive undertook a review of its prison resources in 2002 which assumed a prison population of 8000 in the next decade (Tombs 2005: section 1.37). But this is not the case in every capitalist state in the twenty-first century as shall be shown.

Finland

One country which has fairly dramatically altered its approach to imprisonment is also on a par with Scotland in terms of size. The Nordic country of Finland with a population of 5.21 million has one of the lowest prison rates in Europe with 71 people imprisoned for every 100,000 of the population. This was not always the case, for in the 1950s Finland had one of the highest rates of imprisonment in the world but this has fallen generally consistently in each of the last few decades. This has been the result of a general policy shift by the establishment within Finland. In the 1970s, Finland also had more prisons than the rest of Scandinavia combined.

Unlike Scotland and indeed England Finland has a Criminal Code. This is a fairly common approach in other European countries where all elements of criminal law and procedure are brought together in a single document. The Finnish code dates from 1889 – and has been subsequently amended. Sentencing policy is one of the areas where there was a shift in Finland. The courts can either fine or imprison someone as a criminal sanction. If a fine is regarded as insufficient punishment, a sentence is imposed. However, around 50 per cent of sentences are suspended – with this automatically being the case for sentences under eight months. One of the reasons for this is that prison is not viewed in the same way as in Scottish society, namely, as a place of punitive regime. This policy alteration was carried out with the involvement of academics and civil service and saw an emphasis on rehabilitation of offenders. The Criminal Sanctions Agency, which oversees all sentences, has one of its stated aims 'endeavouring to break the cycle of social exclusion that reproduces crime' (Tombs 2005: section 1.43). However, what of the victims of crime? Are they satisfied with this approach? The point is often made by politicians in Scotland and England that the position of victims should be considered as central to all criminal prosecutions. This actually is the case in Finland.

As in Scotland, most criminal cases are brought by a public prosecutor, although there are still provisions which allow victims to bring their own private prosecutions. This is theoretically possible in Scotland but very rare and difficult to pursue. Further, the victim has a direct role in each stage of the criminal process and a place in court. As part of the criminal trial, the victim can place a request for compensation which is heard at the same time. Or, alternatively, the victim can make a financial claim from the state – a scheme which is one of the most generous in Europe. The philosophy of this is that rather than focus on the punitive sanction on the perpetrator of a crime, the victim gains 'justice' by being involved in the process and gaining an element of financial compensation. This integrated approach is not utilised in the Scottish legal system. Alongside this, the Finnish legal system has expanded on a system of mediation between victim and offender. This began in the mid-eighties in one of the larger cities of Finland, Vantaa. Now there is a system of mediation which can be accessed by around 85 per cent of the population. In the Scots context, mediation can be used in family law disputes, for example, following a divorce or separation to determine a financial settlement or access to children. In Finland, however, it is part of the criminal justice system; that is, a victim of a crime sits with the perpetrator of the crime and an independent mediator to determine an outcome which is acceptable (Iivari 2002).

Under the Finnish system, the police, public prosecutor, victim or offender can choose to refer a case to mediation. From this a contract will be drawn up which will have a remedy to be carried out by the perpetrator. This contract is legally enforceable. Such a process is seen as particularly appropriate for dealing with young offenders but it has been extended to older people. The type of crimes which are most commonly dealt with in this way are assault and battery, and vandalism. The most common remedies through mediation are some form of compensation, either through money or through work. Even the issuing of an apology can be seen as appropriate, or a combination of several of these. Significantly, since the scheme has been introduced and developed, the police have interacted with the model and a large number of referrals come from them.

This mediation scheme is potentially far-reaching – it deals with around 5,000 cases a year – but it has problems. Unlike other jurisdictions (see Norway below), there is not a lot of financial support provided by the state and most mediation offices are fairly small and their resources can be stretched. Moreover, it is not a wholly national system – there are large geographical areas that are not covered at all, albeit this is only a small proportion of the population as a whole. But if the mediation scheme is viewed in the context of the Finnish legal system's approach to penal policy, sentencing and the victims of crime, there is a clearly different approach to criminal justice to that used in Scotland.

It may be argued that there is a cultural difference. For example, there is little lurid reporting of crime within Finnish society – something which is common-place in all media in Britain. Law and order feature in only a limited way in any political debate between the establishment political parties compared to the 'Dutch auction' on punitive criminal justice policies within the Scottish Parliament (albeit this altered slightly in the 2003 Finnish elections where the rightwing True Finns party used a law and order agenda). But such 'cultural difference' is not fixed and ignores that there had been a cultural shift in the course of the last couple of generations – from being one of the highest jailers to being one of the lowest. This shift took a concerted effort by the entire capitalist state within Finland. But even here, this national shift has not been immune to international pressures. So, in recent years, the rate of imprisonment has grown slightly, largely due to drugs offences. Thus, the punitive element of the 'war on drugs', mainly an American export, has a ripple effect even in remote Scandinavia. However, even when this is taken into account, Scotland has adopted the opposite approach to Finland, and reasons for why this may be are examined below.

Norway

Another comparable country in terms of size and location to Scotland is Norway. In many ways, Norway has a more integrated approach to mediation and alternatives to custody than any other European country and, consequently, has maintained low levels of incarceration. Again, Norway has a criminal code dating from the nineteenth century. However, unlike many countries including Scotland, in its criminal court procedure Norway has very flexible rules. In many jurisdictions, lawyers spend years studying rules of evidence and procedural points. If these are not followed this can have a major impact on the trial. Norway does not have this –as a result there is greater lay, that is non- legally trained, involvement in court. Furthermore, Norway has a large lay element in its judiciary at all levels. That is judges do not have to be legally trained to pass judgements in criminal trials. There is some scope for this even in the Scottish legal system. In the lowest criminal court justices of the peace can hear trials for minor offences – they are not qualified but appointed under the aegis of local councils. In Norway, this system goes right to the top of the judiciary.

Imprisonment is an option which can be used for criminal action but, as the statistics indicate, it is not viewed as central to the country's criminal justice system. There is a large use of suspended sentences particularly for offences that have a sentence of no more than one year. Of those actually incarcerated, the Norwegian Criminal Statistics for 1991 indicate the largest number are those who have committed 'other crimes', that is, not violent crimes against the person nor crimes against property but anti-social behaviour like being drunk or dangerous driving or fraud. Alongside this, since the eighties the alternative system of mediation has operated. This system can only work if it is clear the perpetrator is guilty – both the victim and offender agree to it and the state decrees that the offence is not serious enough to warrant immediate imprisonment.

Of significance in developing this policy was the Norwegian criminologist Christie – who examined the whole concept of criminal justice. Thirty years ago, Christie (1976) argued that the state had in effect stolen conflicts between people in order to impose its own power. So, where possible, people should be given their conflicts back in order to determine a solution. Mediation was thus viewed as a 'diversionary' strategy in the criminal justice system – an alternative to court. Immediate focus was also on young people whose involvement with criminal behaviour may have just begun. As in Finland, a pilot scheme began in various regions of Norway. However, unlike that country, a national scheme was established in 1991 and funded centrally by the state. Police or prosecutors can refer cases to mediation and if the scheme is agreed to, and followed, then this disposes of the case. The most commonly referred group are young men between 15 and 17 with the most common offences being shoplifting, theft and vandalism (Miers 2001:46). The remedies involve financial or work compensation. Such has been the success of this scheme that further investigation into the use of mediation in the cases of severe violence was commissioned by the Norwegian Ministry of Justice in 2001. So again, an emphasis on alternatives to a criminal court and a different view on the purposes of sentencing and, indeed, jail results in a much lower level of incarceration.

Different approaches? Many obstacles?

Why, then, in our society are the imprisonment rates double the levels of Finland and Norway? There are clearly a number of factors behind this. It is worthwhile considering the comments of Christie so influential in the mediation model in a recent interview. He argued the 'prison-industrial complex' stemming from America has had 'huge unhealthy consequences for the rest of the globe' (Interview in *New Internationalist* 1996). The imprisonment rates in America are by far the highest in the world with the possible exception of China where statistics are patchy. In 2004, there were 2 million Americans in prison - that is 701 people jailed for every 100,000 people living in the United States *(World Prison Brief*, February 2004 prisonstudies.org). In the 1970s, it was a fraction of this at 110 people for every 100,000. Now it is more than five times the rate of Scotland and ten times that of Norway. This level of imprisonment is obviously big business in the ultimate capitalist state. As Christie points out, you can almost smell industries salivating at the potential money making from the state – the electronics, catering, construction companies all benefit from an endless expansion of prison numbers.

It seems that where America leads Britain follows and not just in illegal military occupations in the Middle East. Although nowhere near American levels - albeit no other state is either, the number of people incarcerated has been dramatically increasing since the 1980s. Britain actually had a fairly low level of imprisonment in the mid twentieth century prior to the Second World War. Across Britain as a whole, the number of prisoners doubled between 1991 and 2003 – from 36,000 to 77,369. This has coincided with a partial privatisation of prison services especially through the use of Private Finance Initiatives. This began with the Major Conservative administration in the early 1990s which contracted the running of several prisons out to the private sector, and this was then deepened by New Labour. There are now 10 private prisons in Britain – one in Scotland at Kilmarnock run by private security firm Premier, the biggest company involved in private prison services. In 2002, the Prison Estates Review recommended that three more private prisons be built in Scotland – this was reduced to one by the Scottish Executive. So a partial explanation can be given by the general take-over of significant elements of the state by private industry in Scotland. More prisoners mean more services need to be provided by private companies. As prisoner numbers are predicted to expand and public spending remains limited, it is only private companies that can fill the void.

But this economic impetus has its political corollary in a hard-line approach from all Scottish and English capitalist politicians and parties towards jail and punitive sentencing. In the nineties, during the genesis of New Labour, Blair as Shadow Home Secretary coined his infamous phrase 'tough on crime, tough on the causes of crime' – it was clear that being tough on crime meant an emphasis on imprisonment. The statement was partially made in response to the then Home Secretary, Michael Howard's, speech that 'prison works'. This approach is now common place amongst all establishment politicians. In outlining the Scottish Executive's legislative programme for 2005-6, Jack McConnell, in a speech to Scottish Parliament on 6 September 2005, made clear the emphasis would be on law and order – or 'justice and respect' as he put it. Reforms were proposed on sentencing and on tightening bail conditions following a horrific crime in Midlothian committed by a person released on bail.

A recent study using Scottish Executive statistics shows that in the last decade although no more people are appearing before court, the rate of imprisonment itself has grown by around 15 per cent (Tombs 2004:8). Between 1993 and 2002, the number of prisoners rose from 5637 to 6404. In that time period increasing use has been made of longer jail sentences and there has been a shift to imprison people for crimes like shoplifting. A clear factor behind this is the political climate in which the legal system operates: the rhetoric of New Labour in government in London and Edinburgh. Another factor is the so-called 'war on drugs' – to some extent another American export. In 2002, 15 per cent of men were in Scottish jails for drug offences and quite incredibly the figure for female prisoners was 29 per cent (Prison Statistics Scotland 2002). As drugs offences – possession and supply – are statutory offences, the penalties are laid down in the *Misuse of Drugs Act 1971*. This means the judiciary has less discretion in determining a penalty as it is laid down in the statute itself.

Significantly, there has been experimentation with alternative legal approaches to drug users with pilot Drug Courts established in Glasgow and Fife in 2001/2. These courts convened by a sheriff can impose number of orders on offenders which relate to drug treatment – but their powers to impose jail sentences are limited. However, some sheriffs have expressed disquiet with this (McIver *et al.* 2003). There are also questions about the resources given over to them. This model has not as of yet been expanded across the whole country. The Scottish Socialist Party has developed a radical drugs policy with the legalisation of cannabis and the medical prescription of heroin that would have a clear effect on these figures. But what use of jail *per se* should socialists support?

It is one of the ironies of Scottish criminal justice that Scotland has one of the largest numbers of alternatives to jail open to the judiciary (Tombs 2005: part 2). These vary from admonishing the guilty (essentially a warning) to community service. There is a developed criminal justice social work system to back many of these remedies up, although like most public services this has been cut back in recent years. Indeed, from 1993 to 2002, there was a 41 per cent increase in non-custody sentences. Even the Scottish Executive at the same time as whipping up the law and order issue have drawn up plans to prevent offenders re-offending with the involvement of communities (Scottish Executive (2003). And yet still, the number of people in prison continues to grow. Is this because of a higher crime rate in Scotland that means level of imprisonment has to remain at very high levels? Internationally, there is no evidence that crime rates affect the level of imprisonment. Countries with similar crime rates to Scotland have lower rates of imprisonment e.g. Sweden. If the Finnish example is looked at, their crime rate is only slightly lower whereas their imprisonment rate as shown is dramatically less (Tombs 2004:13).

It is clear there are contradictory forces at work here and it is not inevitable in capitalist states that there are astronomical levels of imprisonment, although there is a trend in America and countries which are closely in their orbit like Britain (including Scotland) and Eastern Europe. As shown, prison services are now part of the great privatisation auction of the age. Yet smaller capitalist countries have adopted different approaches which seem to engage more with the social aspects of crime and have not increased their prison numbers. Setting the economic and political context of Scotland aside, there is a legal issue which limits the ability to fully develop alternatives to sentencing for Scottish offenders and that is the very strict division between civil and criminal law in both procedure and structure in Scots law. This is despite there being a very large overlap particularly on crime. In essence, civil law regulates the relationships between individuals within a society whereas criminal law sees the state punishing individuals for committing an act which society has deemed to be unacceptable. However, in criminal law as the state takes over the prosecution the individual affected by the crime is removed from the whole process. So the Finnish situation outlined above where the victim has an input at all levels of the trial is impossible in the current Scottish situation. Although a victim can raise an action for damages – this is a civil action which they have to raise themselves through an entirely different court procedure.

As a result the victim can feel completely alienated from the process – all they have is the sentence. How often in the Scottish media is the victim, or their relatives, asked what they think of the sentence passed by the judiciary or their response if a trial collapses? Although the event has a dramatic effect on their life, they are reduced to mere spectators. This was relevant in the Surjit Singh Chhokar case where the family of the murdered man had limited or next to no contact with the prosecutors in the preparation or handling of the case – this was commented on by the official inquiry into the case in 2001. As a result of this alienation, there is a belief that in criminal cases that a punitive jail term is a 'fair' result. In Christie's (1996) words: 'Lawyers steal other people's conflicts: we need to give them back to the people directly concerned'. That is not to say the state should not have a role in prosecuting some crimes. There are types of behaviour that are extremely dangerous and require the state to intervene. Yet it is the Chinese Wall that is erected between state action and the victim's input that causes many problems.

A more radical approach than integrating a civil element into a criminal trial is the removal of criminal behaviour from the courts completely and the introduction of a mediation scheme. As has been shown from the Scandinavian examples, this can involve a victim and perpetrator of crime sitting together and working out a solution. In essence drawing up a contract – a civil remedy which in Scots law is utterly distinct from criminal procedure. Mediation does form part of the Scottish legal system but solely in civil law. It is actively encouraged in family law disputes although it is not compulsory. Complex contract problems particularly in the building industry can be decided on through arbitration – a form of mediation. Yet introducing such measures in the realm of criminal law seems beyond the pale – criminal behaviour needs to be punished by the state or so the argument goes. Following from this, the clearest form of punishment is imprisonment. A partial exception to this is the Children's Panel Hearings where a more collegiate approach is taken when a young person commits a criminal act. As has been shown, the Norwegian model of mediation also initially focused on young people. Perhaps the view is that young people require a degree of protection but for others mediation would seem to be a soft option for committing crime. Yet would making a perpetrator engage with their victim and see the impact that their behaviour has had, and seek to remedy it, not be more beneficial to society?

Conclusion

Christie has criticised a completely 'liberal' approach to crime – often levelled at socialists, i.e., just ignoring the impact of crime on people's lives. He argued (Christie 1976, *New Internationalist* 1996) there must be a reaction to crime – 'These acts must be reacted to otherwise your society is not alive. But who said you react with pain delivery?' What he was arguing was that we should look at social solutions to crime that involve the affected parties as an alternative to punitive, state-led measures. This would allow jail to focus on the small minority of offenders who are truly dangerous or have carried something out that does deserve that kind of punishment.

Frederich Engels once argued that, in the final analysis, the state could be boiled down to bodies of armed men. In the current era, it has been shown that fairly militaristic states like the United States and China have expanded this definition into the 'prison-industrial complex'. Britain to an extent has followed this approach – even Scotland with a range of alternatives to custody has fallen into line. Societies that existed before the state grew so strong under modern capitalism, and certainly before the current integration of big business with all elements of the state, had their own methods of dealing with 'criminal' action. Native Americans and Canadians, Maoris, and African tribes in smaller groups dealt with crime in a more direct way. For example, the African concept of 'ubuntu' in a community meant that when issues of justice were discussed there would be a collective element where a larger group including the victim and offender would discuss how to remedy a particular crime (Anderson 2003). Significantly, many countries are examining these traditions as an alternative to their reliance on state-led remedies, with 'ubuntu' being examined in South Africa.

Could this type of approach be used in the Scottish context? There is a clear cultural and political attachment to prison as a remedy in Scotland – both through the media and the capitalist political parties. The SSP has an obvious role in pointing out the short-sighted and limited approach this offers. In so doing though the SSP should be at the forefront of promoting other remedies which reconnect people with the processes that affect them, including criminal justice and make perpetrators of crime engage with the consequences of their actions. This should cut across the idea of being 'soft' on the impact of crime. Mediation, if properly funded, could become an important element alongside a more integrated approach to civil and criminal procedure that would seek to end the alienation of victims of crime. International examples show that these remedies can have an effect, even in capitalist societies. The level of incarceration in any society tells a story – 'How large a prison population can you have before you change the type of country you live in?' (Christie in *New Internationalist* 1996).

Websites

- Prison Statistics :www.prisonstudies.org
- Restorative Justice resources: www.restorativejustice.org/resources/world/
- Northern Justice Systems: www.explorenorth.com/justice.html

Chapter 13

How Britain's overseas adventures are reshaping justice in Scotland

Richard Haley

"I found myself in the mind of the Masquerade. I saw the world through its eyes. I surveyed its extensive, universal kingdom of fear. Dread for those who oppose, protection for supporters, nightmares for the silent. I saw far across the lands, into the hearts of nations whose heartbeats had accelerated and been taken over by the powers of fear"

Ben Okri (Songs of Enchantment, 1993)

A week before the Christmas of 2002, three Edinburgh men – Algerian expatriates as it happened - were woken by armed police and driven off to places the press described as 'secret locations in Scotland.' A fourth man was arrested later in the day when he turned up at one of the flats where the earlier arrests had been made. Another four men were arrested in London and brought up to those 'secret locations in Scotland.' And then, a ninth man was arrested in Scotland. The men were all charged with offences under the *Terrorism Act* 2000. An MI5 'source' told *Scotland on Sunday* (22 December 2002) that there was a plot to bomb Edinburgh's Hogmanay party. Official police sources flatly denied any 'specific threat.' By the time the men's bail hearings came up on 14 March 2003, it was clear that there was no evidence against them at all. But the Anglo-American invasion of Iraq was just 6 days away. Tony Blair was getting ready to tell Parliament that terrorist groups and the Iraqi regime jointly constituted 'a real and present danger to Britain and its national security.' It would have taken a brave Procurator Fiscal to shrug and drop the charges. So the men went home on police bail but the charges were not dropped until the following December.

Empire and Resistance

One way to gauge the issues that concern the ruling class is to look at the way Parliament passes its time. Between 1980 and 1992, the UK Parliament introduced a new piece of anti-union legislation every two years. With the law behind it, the British ruling class detached its sources of wealth, as far as it could, from the influence of the organised British working class. This was accomplished partly through the continued migration of manufacturing industry out of Britain. Yorkshire folk used to say that 'where there's muck, there's brass.' For the builders of the new economy, keeping muck and brass apart is usually the way to go.

More capital flows in and out of Britain than through any other country in Europe - both the average inflow of foreign investment to the UK and the average outflows from the UK over the period 1991-2002 were larger than for any other European country (UN 2003). The economic power of wealthy Britons can be rooted anywhere on earth, but their political power is still largely dependent on the British state. It hardly matters whether you describe this as post-colonialism, globalisation or imperialism. What matters is that Britain's role in this system is exceptionally well developed.

For the British elite, this is an arrangement filled with enchanting opportunities. The rest of us hardly notice it until it becomes manifest as a deadly threat. People in flight from threat to their lives are moving around the world with unprecedented fluidity. Usually, they have no choice but to move to a neighbouring country where the threat is hardly less than at home. But in the 1980s, refugees began to show up in countries like Britain – countries that are both home to and powerhouse for the global elite. Regulating the flow of people and ideas between the domains of muck and brass has become a key objective of the ruling class. Between 1993 and 2002, the UK Parliament introduced a new piece of anti-refugee or anti-immigration legislation every three years. After 2002, it became an annual event. These new laws exclude refugees from justice unless or until they have obtained some form of protection (asylum, exceptional leave to remain, discretionary leave or humanitarian protection). Something like 6,000 Glasgow refugees are in this predicament. The available statistics are based on the provision of publicly funded support by the National Asylum Support Service (NASS). According to the Home Office, 5,720 people in Glasgow were receiving such support at the end of June 2005. There are probably several hundred Glasgow refugees without such support. Sources from 2003 show 329 people in the area receiving non-NASS support (Asylum-seekers and Refugees in Glasgow, see icar.org.uk/?lid = 4826).

These refugees are the people often referred to as 'asylum-seekers' – a bureaucrat's term that I will not use again in this chapter. The normal word for people in need of refuge is refugee. Before the spin-doctors got their hands on it, the word was applied without qualification to anyone in flight from war or disaster, and it is still used that way as long as the refugee stays out of the nations of brass. We should return it to its full meaning and stop speaking of refugees as if they were maniacs in search of an institution.

The most urgent call that refugees make on the state's sense of justice is their request for protection – a life or death matter. This is decided not by a proper court, but by an adjudicator operating in a para-judicial framework where the burden of proof lies with the refugee, where there is no provision for record-keeping and where accountability is minimal. The authorities possess immense and arbitrary powers over the life of a refugee who has not been granted protection. Such refugees can be sent to a detention centre or jail, separated from their children, or put on a flight out of the country by administrative fiat. These powers are being exercised with increasing brutality. Since the summer of 2005, Glasgow's refugee communities have been terrorised by a series of dawn raids leading to the deportation of whole families.

It is often said that the world changed after '9/11'. For people living in Britain, the world changed seven months earlier, when the *Terrorism Act 2000* came into force on 19 February 2001. The Act means that every government on earth is protected from every people on earth by British law. Its opening section declares that:

The government' means the government of the United Kingdom, of a Part of the United Kingdom or of a country other than the United Kingdom.

It has long been axiomatic on the left – and the not-so-left – that the people of a country hold the right of regime-change there, and that foreign powers have no such right. The *Terrorism Act* stands this principle on its head. Most of the activities necessary to dislodge a government fond of power fall within the Act's definition of terrorism. Action intended to influence a government with the aim of 'advancing a political, religious or ideological cause' constitutes terrorism not only if it involves violence against the person, but also if it involves serious damage to property, or if it endangers a life, or threatens the 'health or safety of the public or a section of the public,' or is intended to interfere with an electronic system. It is hard to imagine how anyone could shift even a mildly obdurate government, or indeed gain its attention, without doing one or another of these things.

The powers contained in the Act are so extensive that the government could find little to add to them after '9/11', despite an irresistible impulse to add something. In the end, they went for the one thing missing from the Act – internment. But rather than antagonise the whole population, they fell back on an old principle: if in doubt, blame the refugees. The internment powers in the *Anti-Terrorism, Crime and Security Act 2001* were limited to foreign citizens who could not be deported because they were at risk of torture. Apart from that, the main thing that changed after '9/11' is that the government began backing up its legal powers with ugly appeals to racism and Islamophobia. The *Terrorism Act 2000* allows the Home Secretary to outlaw any organisation that he believes is 'concerned in' the redefined activity of terrorism. As of November 2005, there are forty organisations currently on the banned list (homeoffice.gov.uk/security/terrorism-and-the-law/terror-ism-act/proscribed-groups?version = 1). They include groups like the Tamil Tigers, the PKK and Kashmiri separatist groups that pose no likely threat to people in Britain, and that have substantial popular support in the areas where they operate. Operations against these movements and their popular base have created vast numbers of refugees. The effect of a banning order on such people is incalculable. A refugee who does not claim association with an organised political movement risks being dismissed as an economic migrant; a refugee cites such an association risks prosecution. It is impossible to guess how many asylum applications have foundered in this 'Catch 22'.

International law has never granted indiscriminate protection to everyone put to flight by politics, and it has never condoned acts that can properly be called terrorism. The 1951 *Geneva Convention* explicitly excludes from protection anyone who has committed war crimes or acts contrary to the purposes and principles of the United Nations. But Britain's re-definition of terrorism threatens to extend the exclusion to anyone who has engaged in any concrete form of opposition politics at all, anywhere in the world. It is a unilateral attempt (paralleled in the US) to round off the Cold War in much the same way that the 1815 Congress of Vienna rounded off the revolutionary and Napoleonic wars – by entrenching established power and putting a freeze on popular regime change.

Like so many instruments of empire, 'new terrorism' was made in Scotland. Professor Paul Wilkinson of the Centre for Studies in Terrorism and Political Violence (CSTPV) at St. Andrew's University served as adviser to Lord Lloyd of Berwick's Inquiry into Legislation Against Terrorism, set up by the Major government, and wrote the second volume of the inquiry's two-volume report (Wilkinson 1996). The CSTPV was founded in 1993 by Bruce Hoffman of the US RAND Corporation, a non-profit research organisation created by the US defence industry. It continues to maintain close links with RAND. Brian Jenkins, Senior Adviser to the President of RAND Corporation, sits on the CSTPV Advisory Council. Many Labour voters might have expected that their government – which came to power promising an 'ethical foreign policy' – would ditch policy advice from outfit with a pedigree like that. Not at all.

The Lloyd of Berwick report became the foundation for the *Terrorism Act 2000*. The expansion of the definition of terrorism to include 'violence' to property was taken straight from the Lloyd report, which in turn borrows almost word for word from the working definition of terrorism used by the FBI since the late 1980s (USDoJ/FBI 1988). And, the focus that Paul Wilkinson put on cross-border 'ideological, political or diplomatic support' for terrorist campaigns helped make the case for a global, politicised view of terrorism. The prohibitions surrounding organisations proscribed under the

Act go far beyond a simple ban on membership. It is an offence to organise, or speak at, a meeting of more than three people if you know that a member of a proscribed organisation will speak at it. If you fail to inform on members of a proscribed organisation, that is an offence. Demonstrating in support of a proscribed organisation or displaying their symbols is an offence. All this has had the effect of criminalising a large portion of the social, political and cultural life of expatriate communities, who often identify strongly with liberation struggles in their homeland.

The Kurdish community in London was an early target of the legislation. Kurdish people and their friends and supporters led the resistance to the new laws and early in 2001 were instrumental in setting up the Campaign Against Criminalising Communities (CAMPACC, www.campacc.org. uk) – a broad-based campaign against anti-terrorism powers and the criminalisation of political activity. SACC was set up two years later in response to the 'terrorism' arrests in Scotland at the end of 2002, and the wave of Islamophobia that accompanied them. The Stop the War Coalition has been committed almost since its inception to defend civil liberties and resist the racist 'backlash'. Then at the end of 2003, the Stop Political Terror campaign (stoppoliticalterror.com) was set up – a Muslim-inspired campaign that is open to everybody. All these groups work together routinely and effectively, and have changed the shape of human rights activism in Britain.

The *Terrorism Act* was not introduced in response to some urgent and deadly threat. On the contrary, the British mainland enjoyed an unusual degree of peace in the last few years on the twentieth century. The new measures were pre-emptive. That is not to say that the government second-guessed '9/11', but rather that it was consciously forging the instruments for a new and more violent relationship between Britain and the world. New Labour sent British forces to war on three occasions prior to '9/11'. Britain bombed Iraq in 1998, Kosovo and Serbia in 1999 and sent troops to Sierra Leone in 2000. It is often said that the current phase of US militarism has come about because US military power exceeds its economic clout. The same remark applies to Britain a *fortiori*. Britain's military strength in relation to the US has declined over the last few decades. It is to be doubted whether Britain could fight even a small war without American help. But Tony Blair is still one of the few world leaders who could decide, if things were to go badly on the battlefield, that he'd destroy the planet instead. Compared to the rest of the world, Britain remains a *bonnie fechter*. And that is just what British players in the global economy need of it. The *Terrorism Act 2000* created the domestic instruments to equip Britain for more of this. If people in Britain go off-message and talk to people overseas with their own voice instead of the voice of the fighter-bomber and the diplomat, they can be jailed for it.

Back in 2000, there was very little sign that the people that Britain bombed might bomb Britain back. The only serious irritant to the state was the anti-capitalist movement, manifested most notably at a series of Mayday demonstrations in London and at the WTO talks in Seattle in 1999. Many people concluded that this movement was indeed the real target of the Act, despite government denials. Five months after the Act came into force in Britain, police in Genoa unleashed massive violence against anti-G8 protestors. Many demonstrators were viciously beaten and one of them – Carlo Giuliani – was murdered. The terrorist attacks on New York and Washington came less than two months after that. It became a commonplace to predict that George Bush and Osama bin Laden would between them squeeze the life from the anti-capitalist movement. Those who said such things must have been surprised to see 400,000 anti-war demonstrators marching through the streets of London the following September, and even more surprised when the biggest mass mobilisation in British history took place on 15 February 2003. The look and feel of the demonstrations was not very different from the look and feel of the anti-capitalist movement.

Hearts and Minds

The Madrid bomb blasts of March 2004 left 191 people dead and 1800 injured. But demonstrations against the bombing quickly turned into demonstrations against the government. They cost Aznar his job and brought the Spanish troops home from Iraq. British counter-terrorism policy since then has been tightly focussed on making sure that neither Blair nor his army would be forced out by a terrorist attack on Britain. As in earlier colonial episodes, an army of privateers and adventurers has settled into Iraq. The first western security firm to establish an office in Iraq was Janusian Security Risk Management Ltd, a security company set up in 2001 by CSTPV founder member David Claridge (see riskadvisory.net/index.php?id = 13). The company claims to have a 'unique relationship with the Centre for the Study of Terrorism and Political Violence at the University of St Andrews, the institution at the forefront of academic research in terrorism and low intensity conflict.'

During the spring of 2004 Bruce Hoffman, founder of CSTPV, was senior advisor to the Constitutional Provisional Authority in Iraq. None of this stops the British press from featuring regular speculation by CTSPV chairman Paul Wilkinson and other CTSPV staff about the domestic terrorist threat. The unwary might suppose them to be independent academics, or even to be people working for peace. Nothing is said in the media about CSTPV's pivotal role in government policy-making or its stake in the exploitation of Iraq.

The attack on domestic dissent has been pressed beyond the refugee community and into the settled community of British Muslims. It is nothing less than the application at home of a counter-insurgency method developed in the British colonies (Clutterbuck 1973) – a method that seeks to play to the state's strengths by applying a military analysis and military ruthlessness to political problems. Used in partnership with New Labour presentational skills, it is a formidable political tool. Any doubts about the militarisation of anti-terrorism policing were abandoned when British and American forces attacked Afghanistan in supposed hot pursuit of the '9/11' terrorists. If you use cluster-bombs as a fast-track extradition process, you have to expect a degree of structural adjustment in your domestic legal arrangements.

Discussion of the 'war on terror' discriminates relentlessly between 'us' and 'them'. 'Our' camp is a place of privilege and safety, where dissent is possible. 'Their' camp is a place of danger. But the strategists of Empire make no such distinction, either in their methodology or in their lives and livelihoods. And, they have made no promise to stick to kid gloves in either camp. The path away from the lifeless chessboard of counter-insurgency theory lies through the lives and experiences of real people, and especially through the many British people – two million of them Muslim – who have ties of family and culture with places overseas. Their involvement in the wider anti-war movement keeps it out of the paternalist dead-end that has trapped sections of the peace movement in the past. That is why the Muslim community has become a particular target of the state. And it is why the state and the media constantly titillate popular racism and Islamophobia. The message to British Muslims is clear – whiten up, or you'll find yourselves in a British enclave of 'their' camp, where the supposed protections of liberal democracy do not apply.

Muslims were put under relentless pressure after the Madrid bombings. No such pressure was put upon followers of other philosophies – nationalism, for instance – that had influenced the bombers. In the end, the Muslim Council of Britain felt compelled to write to every mosque in the country asking them not just to condemn terrorism but to 'observe the utmost vigilance' and to give police 'the fullest co-operation.' It is reminiscent of the tried and tested tactic of encouraging colonies-in-making to invite their occupiers in. Most of the time, the Muslim community handles all this with grace and aplomb, rolling with the punches and refusing to surrender its identity or its sense of justice. But only an idiot would deny that Muslims need all the help they can get.

Cabinet documents leaked in May 2005 revealed a project targeted at the hearts and minds of young British Muslims (*Sunday Times* 30 May 2004). Foreign imams were to be vetted before being allowed into Britain. 'Moderate', home-grown imams would be given government support. There would be funding for 'moderate' Islamic newspapers, television and radio stations. There would be intervention at 'key trigger points.' A briefing paper talked of the need to 'understand the terrorist career path'.

All this was linked to a strategy promoted in government and police circles by Dr Magnus Ranstorp, director of CSTPV at that time. Ranstorp has a clear view of the 'terrorist career path' (Upton 2004). He argues that it begins with spiritual training, then progresses through an 'acclimatisation' phase involving exposure to 'propaganda' about struggles in places such as Algeria and Chechnya. On this view, the whole of Muslim life is fair game for the police, and political activities are objects of particular suspicion. Is this the core of Ranstorp's strategy, or is it just co-lateral damage? His recommendations for government action in the event of a terrorist attack give a clue. He says that the 'psychological ripple effect' of an attack is the key; 'addressing the nation immediately and effectively' is as important as 'the mitigation of physical effects'. Evidently, the political consequences of an attack matter to Ranstorp at least as much as the human cost.

Stories appear in the press regularly about 'extremist' Islamic activity in Scottish universities, particularly in Glasgow and Dundee. They are generally based on information from sources in the security services. Given the government's working model of the 'terrorist career path,' the term 'extremist' could mean anything. Fears sown by these reports have made it harder for student Islamic societies to attract new members. This kind of assault on community activity is deeply felt amongst Muslims. Early in 2005, MI5 launched a well-publicised campaign to recruit 1000 new agents – a huge increase to their existing staff of 2200. Much of the expansion appears to have been targeted on Scotland and reports appeared in the press (*Scotsman* 20 January 2005) of plans for a new 'operational' base in Glasgow - MI5's first permanent base north of the border. Overt surveillance of the Muslim community has also been expanded.

Shortly after the London bombings, plans were announced for new Special Branch units to be set up around the country, modelled on the well-established Muslim Contact Unit already operating in London (*Guardian* 20 July 2005). A number of London Muslims have praised the MCU for being well-informed on the affairs of their community – a refreshing change from the prejudice and ignorance usually shown by the police. But the work of the MCU is based on a protection racket. In the words of a senior police source, 'you protect them against Islamophobia, and work with Muslims to protect them against extremists.' Police say frankly that the MCU engages in 'intelligence-gathering'.

Linking this to the policing of racist attacks is deeply unethical. It undermines community solidarity and encourages people to buy in to the policing of political activity. Police in Scotland are taking this policy a step further under a scheme being piloted in Tayside. A 'community contact unit' staffed by special branch officers has been sent into secondary schools in the area. According to John Vine, Chief Constable of Tayside, 'what we have to change is the mindset which questions whether it is appropriate to gather intelligence in schools' (*Scotsman* 8 October 2005).

To Deter and Disrupt

Government efforts to treat the law as 'war by other means' are creating deep rifts in the British establishment. So far, conflict between the executive and the judiciary has centred on the government's tooth and nail fight to scrap the right of *habeas corpus*. The 17 or so refugees from North Africa and Jordan on whom the Home Office has tested its strength have had to run a gauntlet reminiscent of *Les Miserables*. They were initially detained under the *Anti-Terrorism Crime and Security Act 2001*, which allowed the Home Secretary to order the internment of foreign nationals if he 'suspected' them of 'links' with terrorism, but was unable to deport them because they were at risk of torture. The men were taken to high-security prisons, but no charges were brought against them, and they were never questioned by police.

Internment was ruled unlawful by the Law Lords in December 2004. Then, in March 2005, a new law – the *Prevention of Terrorism Act 2005* - was rushed through Parliament allowing the Home Secretary to impose various forms of house arrest on anyone (British citizen or foreign national) he 'suspects' of 'terrorism-related activity'. Orders of this kind were placed on a number of the former internees. They are currently back in jail as a result of a government attempt to deport them, notwithstanding the risk of torture they face if returned to their home countries. Almost all the former internees have experienced serious mental health problems as a result of their treatment in Britain.

The effect of all this has been devastating for their friends and families and for the little community of refugees they live amongst, and salutary for the wider public – especially the Muslim public.

In the aftermath of the London bombings, the government tried to change the law to allow police to hold terrorist suspects for 90 days before bringing charges (see *Terrorism Bill*, as printed on 3 November 2005). Pre-charge detention had previously been limited to 14 days for terrorism suspects and just 36 hours for people suspected of 'ordinary' offences. Three-month detention would have been qualitatively different. It would have accelerated the tendency of the police to arrest people first and look for evidence afterwards, and it would have added a strong punitive element to detention. In other words, it would have been internment by another name. In the event, MPs rejected the proposal after an intense lobbying campaign by civil liberties groups. It was Blair's first parliamentary defeat. But the House of Commons approved detention for 28 days – still a very long time to spend in a police cell without knowing the charge against you.

Police have in the meantime been applying a makeshift internment policy of their own with very little fuss. Section 57 of The *Terrorism Act 2000* makes it an offence to 'possess an article in circumstances which give rise to a reasonable suspicion that ... possession is for a purpose connected with the commission, preparation or instigation of an act of terrorism.' It makes suspicion the basis not just for arrest, but also for conviction. The burden of proving that a 'suspicious' article is unconnected with terrorism is placed upon the defendant. Any article will do, however, ordinary – it is the circumstances that are said to make it suspicious. This catch-all offence is used regularly as a holding charge. South of the border, people are often held in jail for a year or more on a Section 57 charge while police look for evidence of a real offence. Scottish law provides a degree of protection against this. The 110-day rule limits the length of time for which a person can be held before the start of a trial. The Algerian 'terrorist suspects' charged in Scotland under Section 57 were bailed when the prosecution found themselves without a case at the end of the 110-day period. If the men had been charged south of the border, they would be probably have been kept in jail until an opportune moment arose to release them without any publicity embarrassing to the government.

Extradition provides another means for the state and its friends to persecute people unlikely to be convicted in a British court. The *Extradition Act 2003* allows people to be extradited to the USA without any opportunity for the evidence against them to be heard in Britain. Babar Ahmad, a British citizen, is facing extradition under this process for offences under US law that he allegedly committed while running a website from Britain (for more information, see freebabarahmad.com). At a hearing in May 2005, the judge, while allowing the extradition, noted that 'the defendant is a British subject alleged to have committed offences which, if the evidence were available, could have been prosecuted in this country'. Babar Ahmad cannot contest the evidence against him, but he is appealing against the extradition on human rights grounds.

There have been many hundreds of terrorism arrests since '9/11', but only a handful of convictions for terrorism. Mike Todd, Manchester's chief constable and spokesman for the Association of Chief Police Officers on terrorism, told the Commons Select Committee on Home Affairs (Minutes, House of Commons Select Committee on Home Affairs, 8 July 2004) that we should not worry about this. 'I do not necessarily regard that as a failure. Often it is a disruption, a deterrent,' he said. When pressed for clarification, he used a preposterous fairy-tale of his own devising to illustrate the difference between intelligence and evidence. Common sense suggests that drag-net operations fuelled by rumour – intelligence-led operations, in police terminology – are unlikely to hinder a serious terrorist. On the other hand, they are likely to be quite effective at deterring and disrupting political activity, whether or not the immediate targets are activists. Activism is a step towards terrorism in the eyes of policy advisors like Ranstorp, so it should not surprise anyone to find the police acting in this way. It hardly matters whether or not individual officers, even at a senior level, appreciate the effect of their actions. The multi-agency intelligence assessments (Minutes of the House of Commons Select Committee on Home Affairs, 8 July 2004) that trigger anti-terrorism operations are held behind closed doors. There is no possibility of any check being applied to their institutional predispositions, and it would be safe to guess that there is not much to prevent one agency or another injecting 'intelligence' calculated to achieve purposes unconnected with crime prevention.

The 'disrupt and deter' strategy has been extended beyond the Muslim and refugee communities into the wider field of opposition politics. In the months leading up to the 2005 G8 Summit at Gleneagles, police, government and media colluded in a sustained campaign to scare people away. People attending demonstrations around Scotland in the days immediately prior to the summit suffered a multi-dimensional assault of police disinformation, provocation and outright brutality. A number of people travelling to and from Scotland were questioned under the *Terrorism Act*, and hundreds of people were arrested under other laws. Despite all this, and despite the deployment of helicopter-borne riot police at Gleneagles itself, at least 10,000 people gathered there for a peaceful protest on 6 July. The London bombers struck on the following day.

The anti-capitalist and anti-war movements have not been scared from the streets. Many tens of thousands of anti-war protestors marched through London on 26 September 2005, and 2000 marched through Edinburgh on 12 November. But, the *Terrorism Bill*, currently (December 2005) going through Parliament, contains the most serious challenge to the movement so far. The Bill seeks to make it an offence to encourage the public to commit acts of terrorism. Terrorism means 'new terrorism', as defined in the *Terrorism Act* 2000. The 'public' means any public in the world. Glorification of actions in the 'past, present or future' is taken to be a form of encouragement. This makes any serious discussion of resistance to imperialism – and much else besides - fair game for surveillance, harassment and possibly prosecution. It is hard to see how this can be squared with Britain's obligations under *Resolution 42/159* of the UN General Assembly. This landmark resolution condemning terrorism was passed in December 1987 with just two countries voting against it (the United States and Israel) and one abstention (Honduras). It includes a clause saying:

> *...nothing in the present resolution could in any way prejudice the right to self-determination, freedom and independence, as derived from the Charter of the United Nations, of peoples forcibly deprived of that right referred to in the Declaration on Principles of International Law concerning Friendly Relations and Co-operation among States in accordance with the Charter of the United Nations, particularly peoples under colonial and racist regimes and foreign occupation or other forms of colonial domination,*

nor, in accordance with the principles of the Charter in conformity with the above-mentioned Declaration, the right of these peoples to struggle to this end and to seek and receive support.

Parliament's Joint Committee on Human Rights (2005) has already drawn attention to the problems created by building new legislation on top of a broad and politicised definition of terrorism. In its report, it recommended that any new offences along the lines of the proposed ban on 'encouraging' or 'glorifying' terrorism should be decoupled from the definition of terrorism contained in the *Terrorism Act 2000*.

Challenging the Security State

The most obvious course of action to reduce the risk of terrorist attacks on Britain is to pull British troops out of the Middle East, abstain from further anti-people interference in the region and call a halt to the escalating militarisation of Britain's role in the world. The police nevertheless have a duty to prevent acts of mass murder and acts of racism. They are hampered in both these tasks by a deeply politicised anti-terrorism policy. The terrorism laws have created new, political, offences. They are more likely to drive people to terrorism than to help police catch bombers. Their function is not crime prevention, but political control. Police officers make day-to-day operational judgements based on their assumptions about the political climate. Conversely, the police and the courts hand key decisions over to the secret state, where they are beyond the reach of public scrutiny, but within the reach of influences from security agencies around the world. The police have been deeply penetrated by the counter-insurgency culture. The problem is likely to prove as serious and as deep-rooted as the institutional racism unearthed by the 1999 MacPherson report into police handling of the Stephen Lawrence murder.

The repeal of the terrorism laws is the indispensable first step to honest policing. Actions that are illegal under the ordinary law are best investigated and prosecuted under the ordinary law; actions that are legal under the ordinary law are best not prosecuted at all. We need a single justice system, not one system for citizens and another for non-citizens. And we need to reject secret courts and secret para-judicial hearings. If justice cannot be seen to be done, it is a safe bet that it is not being done.. We often hear about 'intelligence-led operations'. We should remember that the invasion of Iraq was an 'intelligence-led operation.'

In the imperial heartlands, the war on terror is a war on freedom of expression. In this climate, to refer to our parliaments as talking-shops is by no means to belittle them. For people of the left who are elected to Parliament – whether at Holyrood, Westminster or Strasbourg – the first duty is to speak out in defiance of authoritarianism and injustice. If the so-called 'glorification' clause of the current *Terrorism Bill* becomes law, this duty will be an especially heavy one. Westminster MPs are generally protected from prosecution over anything they say in Parliament but Holyrood MSPs are not. But serious debate about the affairs of Iraq, Palestine and many other places will be stillborn if parliamentarians accept a ban on saying anything likely to encourage people engaged in struggle against their government.

Justice will not be won by quiet argument. The problem does not end with the law. The police have been deeply penetrated by the counter-insurgency culture. Nothing less than the kind of root-and-branch reform attempted in response to the MacPherson report is likely to reverse this. The state is careful to heed the representations of human rights campaigners and community groups. The problem is that it formulates their concerns in the weakest possible way. It sets up straw men, then it either blows them down or invites them to take a seat at the table of tokenism (House of Commons Home Affairs Committee 2005). In Britain, it seems, the road to fascism is paved with thoughtful parliamentary committee work. Despite the race for new legislation, existing laws are not enforced to anywhere near their full extent. The wide powers of the *Terrorism Act 2000* have mainly been brought to bear on enemies of the government who are isolated enough to be picked off, and on unlucky folk who happen to have encountered over-keen policemen. The balance of forces decides which parts of the law are enforceable. We should not simply withdraw from political spaces that the government targets. And we should not comply with laws that deny our basic human rights if we can help it. For groups like CAMPACC and SACC, campaigns for civil liberties are above all campaigns in defence of the right of solidarity. We need to insist on solidarity across borders, across industries and across lines of race and community. That way, another world is possible. In the words of Babar Ahmad: 'Today it is my turn. Tomorrow it will be your turn'.

Conclusions and Recommendations

- Britain's current anti-terrorism laws and the *Extradition Act 2003* must be repealed;
- Any move to repeal or erode Britain's *Human Rights Act* must be rejected;
- Any form of detention without trial must be rejected, as must any other serious sanctions imposed without trial;
- The banning and blacklisting of organisations must be rejected;
- Complicity in torture is illegal under British, Scottish and International law, and these laws must be enforced;

- People must not be deported for political dissent, whether they are British citizens or not;
- Any laws built upon a wide, politicised definition of terrorism like that contained in the *Terrorism Act 2000* must be rejected;
- Any move toward secret courts or removal of the right to trial by jury must be rejected. Vulnerable defendants and witnesses may sometimes need protection, but this cannot justify systematic secrecy;
- International agreements obliging countries to enact oppressive anti-terrorism measures must be unravelled. We need to build a people's security, not a global security state;
- All new legislation must be viewed in the light of state efforts to criminalise political activity and so we must be ready to resist the erosion of hard-won rights;
- Any move to erode Scotland's 110-day rule must be rejected;
- When institutions that promote human rights come under attack, they must be defended - whatever the pretext for the attack; and
- An effective Scottish Human Rights Commission must be set up.

Chapter 14

Conclusion

Gregor Gall

The chapters contained in this collection do not pretend to be anything like the last word on the outlining a radical totality for reshaping justice and the justice system in Scotland. For a start, not all salient areas were intended to be covered in this collection, for that would have been a task far beyond the resources available to this project. Then, there were, unfortunately, some invited contributors who were unable to find the time and space to write their chapters. And, finally, the contributors here have put forward assessments and ideas which are grounded and forthright but not necessarily definitive positions for all time to come. Nonetheless, the contributors have begun to search and lay out serious alternative solutions, and in this, they should be highly commended. The common threads of the approaches the contributors have taken are that the neo-conservatism of past Conservative and present Labour administrations has had ample time to demonstrate its ineffectiveness, injustice and redundancy; the issues afflicting individuals, communities and justice in society run deep as do their sources and this requires fundamental reform; and that one-sided 'one size fits all' solution are demonstrably inadequate. On top of this, the way in which 'justice' and 'injustice' are conceived is a matter of politics, philosophy and worldviews. Clearly, those with social values of compassion and fairness for the mass of ordinary citizens and the disadvantaged through a socialised democracy and economy begin from a quite different starting points from those who make issues of crime and justice subservient and beholden to economic growth and neo-liberalism. But as was made clear at the outset, the purpose of this collection has been to allow a critical but productive engagement with the processes, outcomes and institutions of crime and justice.

So in the cases of deployment of prison, the police and incarceration, the contributors do not reject these outright or out of hand. Rather, we can detect the persuasive argument for a much more selective and targeted approach to their usage, where both the conditions and the purpose of their usage is significantly changed. For example, Tombs and McKerrell argued for a diminution in the use of prison while Sheridan and Tasker argued for its use with regard to specific crimes and offences. These positions are not incompatible – rather they are sensitive to specific situations and the notion of using the law to establish and reinforce our desired moral codes. What all positions here represent is the view that if prison is to have a productive role then the appropriate conditions for this must be understood and not undermined by a knee-jerk, indiscriminant usage. The backdrop to these contributions is a widespread recognition that, to mimic the Tories' 1979 iconic election poster, 'prison isn't working'. But it is not just prison that isn't working. In his chapter, Dailly highlighted the improbability of the individual citizen gaining civil justice, and pointed to the need for a new institution, a civil tribunal and working to set criteria. Both Haley and McManus also pointed to the need to establish permanent commissions to protect individuals from injustice and to promote justice. In their contributions, Fairweather and McKerrell suggested a turn to allow more and different types of agencies to play a role in the justice system – Fairweather, families and McKerrell, mediation. In all the contributions, consideration has been given to the institutions, processes, values, and outcomes of the existing justice system. Creating a better justice system, of course, requires resources. Some may be additional while others maybe internally redirected from those existing resources. Either way, a new political will is needed to allow this and new values to exercise themselves over our justice system.

One of the most stimulating points to emerge, particularly from the contributions of Baldassara and McKerrell, is that those subject – that is, the ordinary citizens - to the justice and policing systems should have a degree of control over determining what they are subject to and how they are subject to it. What are the specific advantages of this? Aside from increasing the degree of popular democracy in Britain through eroding the monopoly of control and expertise held by the state and legal profession in this regard, a far higher level of respect for, and effectiveness and legitimacy of, the justice system would ensue - the very characteristics that are largely missing at the moment. This is because consultation and participation by the subjects of the justice system in the determination of the justice and policing systems would lead to a manifest sense of influence over the justice and policing systems. 'Empowerment' is an over- and ill-used term but this is what it could come to mean, forming a part of a society of popular, or people's, democracy.

Another issue to emerge is why should statist notions of justice, that is state-centred and structured justice systems, always prevail? In this sense, the traditional point of the left in arguing that the (capitalist) state is often one of the main problems with regard to justice may have some resonance. So, again, can we envisage structured and informed popular participation in justice systems which leads to widespread popular control and legitimacy? Can we have a devolved system of justice that operates at a much lower level than the nation state? These issues are raised merely as questions for there a host of other considerations to be made here, but we need at base to be able to imagine and construct possibilities outside our well-worn conventions.

Without privileging any notion of a superiority of any or all things 'Scottish', the devolved settlement should be at least capable of producing 'Scottish' solutions to 'Scottish' problems – policy developed in Scotland utilising available knowledge from elsewhere to tackle the problems as they are presently configured and as we find them here. It is clear that a roadblock of political will exists here. To realise these possibilities, a fortuitous environment would be the further advance of the various components on the left of the rainbow politics in Scotland in the 2007 Holyrood elections. The same might be said for the prospects of pro-independence parties gaining a majority in the Scottish Parliament. What would conventionally be termed further 'political fragmentation' would open up space for not merely debate but space for leverage and action. So either under external pressure – for example, the Greens agitating - or through internal compromise – for example, the Greens in a governing coalition - the current roadblock represented by the Labour-Liberal Democrats could be broken. This would appear to be the kind of momentous change that would either force new Labour into policy reversals or see new Labour standby and watch its neo-conservative legacy being eroded. It is the hope of this conclusion that such ideas as represented in this collection would be able to flourish – and have a positive, manifest outcome – in such a reconfigured political scene.

References

Anderson, A. (2003) Restorative Justice, the African Philosophy of Ubuntu and the 'Diversion of Criminal Prosecution' School of Law, University of South Africa.

Ashworth, A. (2003) 'Sentencing and Sensitivity: A Challenge for Research' in Zedner, L. and Ashworth, A. (eds.) The Criminological Foundations of Penal Policy, Oxford University Press, Oxford.

Ashworth, A. and Hough, M. (1996) 'Sentencing and the climate of opinion' Criminal Law Review, November, pp761-848.

Austin, J., Irwin, J. and Kubrin, C. (2003) 'It's about time: America's imprisonment binge' in Blomberg, T. and Cohen, S. (eds.) Punishment and Social Control, Aldine De Gruyter, New York.

Baldwin, J. (2002) Lay and Judicial Perspectives on the Expansion of the Small Claims Regime, Department of Constitutional Affairs, London.

Blomberg, T., Bales, W. and Reed, K. (1993) 'Intermediate Punishment: Redistributing or Extending Social Control?' Crime, Law and Social Change, 19:187-201.

Blomberg, T. and Lucken, K. (1994) 'Stacking the Deck by Piling Up Sanctions: Is Intermediate Punishment Destined to Fail?' Howard Journal, 33/1:62-80.

Blomberg, T.(2003) 'Penal Reform and the Fate of "Alternatives"' in Blomberg, T. and Cohen, S. (eds.) Punishment and Social Control, Aldine De Gruyter, New York.

Carlen, P. and Tombs, J. (2006, forthcoming) 'Reconfigurations of Penality: The On-Going Case of The Women's Imprisonment and Reintegration Industries' Theoretical Criminology.

Chapman, B., Mirrlees-Black, C. and Brown, C. (2002) Improving Public Attitudes to the Criminal Justice System: The Impact of Information, Home Office Research Study 245, London, Home Office.

Christie, N. (1976) 'Conflicts as Property' British Journal of Criminology, 17/1:1-15.

Christie, N. (1996) 'Crime and civilization: Interview with Nils Christie' New Internationalist 282, available at newint.org/issue282/crime.htm .

Clutterbuck, R (1973) Riot and Revolution in Singapore and Malaya 1945-1963, Faber and Faber, London.

Currie, E. (1993) Reckoning: Drugs, The Cities And The American Future, Hill and Wang, New York.

Dailly, M. (2004) 'Robbing the poor?', Journal of the Law Society of Scotland, available online: journalonline.co.uk/article.aspx?id = 1001229 .

Davis, A. (2003) Are Prisons Obsolete? Seven Stories Press, New York.

Dunbar, I. and Langdon, A. (1998) Tough Justice: Sentencing and Penal Policies in the 1990s, Blackstone, London.

DWP (2005) Households Below Average Income dataset, DWP, London, available online: scotland.gov.uk/Publications/2005/06/07115348/53542 .

HCW and PC (2004) The Work of the Health and Safety Commission and Executive, House of Commons Work and Pensions Committee, HC 456, available online: publications.parliament.uk/pa/cm200304/cmselect/cm-worpen/456/45602.htm .

Hough, M., Millie, A. and Jacobson, J. (2003) The Decision to Imprison: Sentencing and the Prison Population, Penal Reform Trust, London.

House of Commons Home Affairs Committee (2005) Terrorism and Community Relations, Report of the House of Commons Home Affairs Committee, April, Stationary Office, London.

HSE (2004a) Statistics of Occupational Safety, Ill-health and Enforcement Action, 2003/04, HSE Statistics Co-ordination Unit.

HSE (2004b) A strategy for workplace health and safety in Great Britain to 2010 and beyond, Health and Safety Executive, hse.gov.uk/aboutus/hsc/strategy2010 .

HSE (2005a) Statistics of Occupational Safety, Ill-health and Enforcement Action, 2004/05, HSE Statistics Co-ordination Unit.

HSE (2005b) 'Offences and Penalties Report- a statement by Justin Mc-Cracken' hse.gov.uk/enforce/off0405/introduction.htm .

Hughes Commission (1980) Report of the Royal Commission on Legal Services in Scotland, HMSO, London.

Hutton, N. (2004) 'Beyond Populist Punitiveness' Punishment and Society, 7/3:243-258.

IDRWG (2000) Improving Debt Recovery Working Group report, available online: govanlc.com/IDRWG .

Iivari, J. (2002) 'Victim-offender mediation in Finland' in Victim-Offender Mediation in Europe, Making Restorative Justice work, The European Forum for Victim-Offender Mediation and Restorative Justice (ed.), Leuven University Press, Leuven, pp193-210, available at pfi-rj.mooball.net/resources/docs/ivari/download .

Jamieson, C. MSP (2000) 'Health and Safety is a Holyrood Issue' The Citizen, Issue 13, (thecitizen.org.uk/articles/vol2/article13a.htm)

JHA/DWP (2006) Joint Home Affair/Department of Work and Pensions Select Committee, Draft Corporate Manslaughter Bill, First Joint Report of Session 2005/06, parliament.the-stationery-ffice.co.uk/pa/cm200506/cmselect/cmworpen/540 /54002.htm .

JCHR (2005) Counter–Terrorism Policy and Human Rights: Terrorism Bill and related matters, Report of the Joint Committee on Human Rights, London.

Jolowicz, J. (2003) 'Adversarial and Inquisitorial Models of Civil Procedure' International and Comparative Law Quarterly, 52/2:281-295.

Lipsey, M. and Wilson, D. (1998) 'Effective Intervention for Serious Juvenile Offenders' in Loeber, R. and D. Farrington (eds) Serious and Violent Juvenile Offenders: Risk Factors and Successful Interventions, Sage, Thousand Oaks, CA.

Mathieson, T. (2000) Prison on Trial, Waterside Press, second English edition, Winchester.

McIvor, G., Eley, S., Malloch, M. and Yates, R. (2003) Establishing Drug Courts in Scotland: Early Experiences of the Pilot Drug Courts in Glasgow and Fife, Scottish Executive, Edinburgh.

McKay, R and Campbell, T. (2001) Indictment: Trial by Fire, Canongate, Edinburgh.

Miers, D. (2001) An International Review of Restorative Justice, Crime Reduction Research Series paper 10, Home Office, London.

OSIJ (2005) International Standards on Legal Aid, Open Society Justice Initiative, available online: justiceinitiative.org/db/resource2/fs/?file_id = 16109 .

Paterson, F. and Tombs, J. (1998) Social Work and Criminal Justice: The Impact of Policy, Stationery Office, Edinburgh.

Petersilia, J. and Turner, S. (1990) 'Comparing Intensive and Regular Supervision for High Risk Probationers' Crime and Delinquency, 36/1:87-111.

Redono, S., Sanchez-Meca, J. and Garridon, V. (2002) 'Crime Treatment in Europe: a Review of Outcome Studies' in McGuire, D. (ed.) Offender Rehabilitation and Treatment, Wiley, Chichester.

Samuel, E. (1988) In the Shadow of the Small Claims Court, Legal Studies Research Findings No.18,

Scottish Office, available online: scotland.gov.uk/cru/resfinds/lsf18-00.htm .

SCC (2003) Knowledge of Consumer Rights in Scotland, Scottish Consumer Council, at: scotconsumer.org.uk/publications/reports/reports03/rp03know.pdf .

SCC (2005) The Civil Justice System in Scotland- a case for review? Scottish Consumer Council, available online: scotconsumer.org.uk/publications/reports/documents/rp11civil.pdf .

SCS (2005) Annual Report, 2004/05, Scottish Courts Service, available online: scotcourts.gov.uk/library/annual_reports/archive.asp .

Scottish Executive (2001) Adult Literacy and Numeracy in Scotland, available online: scotland.gov.uk/library3/lifelong/alan-00.asp .

Scottish Executive (2002a) Prisons' Estates Review, Scottish Executive, Edinburgh.

Scottish Executive (2002b) Civil Judicial Statistics, Scottish Executive, Edinburgh.

Scottish Executive (2003) Supporting Safer, Stronger Communities: Scotland's Criminal Justice Plan, Scottish Executive, Edinburgh.

Scottish Executive (2004) Supporting Safer, Stronger Communities: Scotland's Criminal Justice Plan, Scottish Executive, Edinburgh.

Scottish Executive (2005) Corporate Homicide – Expert Group Report, Scottish Executive scotland.gov.uk/Publications/2005/11/14133559/35592 .

Scottish Prison Service (2006) Prison Projections, SPS, Edinburgh.

Spencer, F. (2004a) Engaging With The Public Interest In Criminal And Youth Justice, Scottish Council Foundation, Edinburgh.

Spencer, F. (2004b) The Public Interest: Fairness in Criminal and Youth Justice, Scottish Council Foundation, Edinburgh.

Stead, M. (2002) What Do The Public Really Feel About Non-Custodial Penalties?, Rethinking Crime and Punishment Briefing, Esmée Fairbairn Foundation, London.

Tombs, J. (2003) The Chance For Change: A Study of the Throughcare Centre Edinburgh Prison, SPS Occasional Paper Series, No 4, Scottish Prison Service, Edinburgh.

Tombs, J. (2004) A Unique Punishment: Sentencing and the Prison Population in Scotland, Scottish Consortium on Crime and Criminal Justice, Edinburgh.

Tombs, J. (2005) Reducing the prison population: penal policy and social choices, Scottish Consortium on Crime and Criminal Justice, Edinburgh.

Tonry, M. (2003) 'Reducing the Prison Population' in Tonry, M. (ed.) Confronting Crime: Crime control policy under New Labour, Willan, Cullompton.

United Nations (2003) World Investment Report, United Nations, New York, available at globalpolicy.org/socecon/ffd/fdi/2003/wirlight.pdf .

Upton, J. (2004) 'In the streets of Londonistan' London Review of Books, 26/2.

USDoJ/FBI (1988) Terrorism in the United States, 1988, Terrorist Research and Analytical Center, Counterterrorism Section, Criminal Investigative Division,

United States Department of Justice/FBI, Washington, December 31.

Wilkinson, P. (1996) Inquiry into Legislation Against Terrorism, Vol. 2, Lord Lloyd of Berwick.

Woolf, L. (1995) Access to Justice: Interim Report to the Lord Chancellor on the civil justice system in England and Wales, summary available online: dca.gov.uk/civil/interfr.htm .

Woolfson, C and Beck, M. (1999) 'The Scottish Safety Anomaly' Scottish Critical Policy Studies, Faculty of Social Sciences, University of Glasgow